HADDON

War in Kurt Vonnegut's
Slaughterhouse-Five

D0927291

Other Books in the Social Issues in Literature Series:

Social Issues in Literature

War in Kurt Vonnegut's *Slaughterhouse-Five*

Claudia Durst Johnson, Book Editor

GREENHAVEN PRESS
A part of Gale, Cengage Learning

GALE
CENGAGE Learning

Detroit • New York • San Francisco • New Haven, Conn • Waterville, Maine • London

Christine Nasso, *Publisher*
Elizabeth Des Chenes, *Managing Editor*

© 2011 Greenhaven Press, a part of Gale, Cengage Learning

For more information, contact:
Greenhaven Press
27500 Drake Rd.
Farmington Hills, MI 48331-3535
Or you can visit our Internet site at gale.cengage.com

For product information and technology assistance, contact us at

Gale Customer Support, 1-800-877-4253
For permission to use material from this text or product, submit all requests online at
www.cengage.com/permissions

Further permissions questions can be emailed to permissionrequest@cengage.com

Articles in Greenhaven Press anthologies are often edited for length to meet page requirements. In addition, original titles of these works are changed to clearly present the main thesis and to explicitly indicate the author's opinion. Every effort is made to ensure that Greenhaven Press accurately reflects the original intent of the authors. Every effort has been made to trace the owners of copyrighted material.

Cover photograph copyright Mickey Adair/Hulton Archive/Getty Images.

LIBRARY OF CONGRESS CATALOGING-IN-PUBLICATION DATA

War in Kurt Vonnegut's Slaughterhouse-five / Claudia Durst Johnson, Book Editor.
    p. cm. -- (Social issues in literature)
    Includes bibliographical references and index.
    ISBN 978-0-7377-5817-7 (hardcover) -- ISBN 978-0-7377-5818-4 (pbk.)
    1. Vonnegut, Kurt. Slaughterhouse-five. 2. War in literature. I. Johnson, Claudia Durst, 1938-
    PS3572.O5S6387 2011
    813'.54--dc22
                                                            2010054417

Printed in the United States of America
    2 3 4 5 6   15 14 13 12 11
FD320

Y 813.54 War

Contents

Chapter 1: Background on Kurt Vonnegut

   Both of Vonnegut's parents and their extended families immigrated to the United States from Germany. After working in public relations and journalism, Vonnegut became a literary figure and a popular culture icon.

   When Vonnegut was in his eighties, the bombing of Dresden continued to haunt him, especially as war raged in Iraq and Afghanistan.

   In this interview Vonnegut comments on his experiences, including the World War II bombing of Dresden, Germany; his reception as a writer; and his philosophy as a novelist.

Chapter 2: *Slaughterhouse-Five* and War

   The fantasy of the planet Tralfamadore is the means through which *Slaughterhouse-Five* protagonist Billy Pilgrim comes to terms with the cruelty of civilization, which is exemplified and amplified by war.

According to Vonnegut, war persists in the past and the present. Time travel allows a brief escape from its overwhelming reality.

Chapter 3: Contemporary Perspectives on War

Introduction

In July 2010, US Army staff sergeant Shane Courville spoke to reporter Heidi Vogt of *The Contra Costa Times* about a battle in Afghanistan on October 3, 2009. He described how he had put dead soldiers into body bags and left them outside an aid station, running out of bags after the first four soldiers. Sixty-four years earlier, in late February 1945, Kurt Vonnegut (now a well-known author), was a German prisoner of war. After the Allied firebombing of Dresden, Germany, he was ordered to look for corpses and pile them into a horse-drawn wagon. The two stories, separated by time, geography, and political justification, are virtually the same, highlighting the never-ending atrocities and countless casualties of war.

Vonnegut emphasizes this theme in his novel *Slaughterhouse-Five* through meaningful references to several wars in history, chiefly World War II but also the Children's Crusade of 1212, the American Civil War, and the Vietnam War, which was raging as Vonnegut wrote the novel. He introduces the Children's Crusade first: In Chapter 1 Mary O'Hare, a nurse and the wife of his war buddy Bernard O'Hare, explodes at Vonnegut, accusing him of planning to write a book romanticizing a war (World War II) fought by "babies." That night, Bernard leaves a nineteenth-century history of the crusade on Vonnegut's bedside table. The American Civil War enters the novel when the character Edgar Derby, a former schoolteacher, sits by the bed of the delirious protagonist, Billy Pilgrim, reading Stephen Crane's antiwar novel *The Red Badge of Courage*. The action in Crane's book could apply to any war, but descriptions of the terrain and war strategy clearly identify the subject as the Battle of Chancellorsville during the Civil War. It, too, was fought by children (which the United Nations has now defined as anyone under the age of eighteen).

The primary setting of *Slaughterhouse-Five* is the World War II Battle of the Bulge, fought by adolescents on both sides. Hitler launched his westward surge in the dead of winter, sending his "Hitler Youth," boys ranging in age from sixteen to nineteen, into combat. The young American soldiers in the 106th infantry division wandered aimlessly in confusion, eating snow out of desperation. Many fled, not knowing where they were going. Vonnegut was caught up in the retreat almost as soon as he was deployed in mid-December 1944. More than 6,800 soldiers were captured by the Germans, including the men in Vonnegut's unit, who surrendered. Vonnegut and three other men escaped and slogged through the woods, hoping to find Americans, but were recaptured. Without food or sleep, they were marched sixty miles eastward to a railway station. For four days afterward, they were packed in unheated railway cars. The prisoners were taken to Dresden and put to work in slaughterhouses that had storage cellars far underground. Though not a military target, Dresden was bombed for four days by the Allies beginning on February 13, 1945. The incendiaries created temperatures of up to 1,000 degrees Fahrenheit on the ground, and most of the people were killed. Vonnegut survived in a meat locker.

Slaughterhouse-Five was published in 1969, eight years after the Americans joined the Vietnam War and six years before the war officially ended. When the Communist North Vietnamese invaded South Vietnam in 1961, the United States, hoping to stop the spread of communism, became actively involved in what was essentially a civil war. In 1964 the US bombed North Vietnam, and Congress gave President Lyndon Johnson the authority to wage an undeclared and unprovoked war on North Vietnam and the Viet Cong rebels in the South. American antiwar rallies escalated, with 35,000 people marching on Washington in November 1965. In 1968, the year Vonnegut finished writing his book on war, more than one thousand US troops were being killed every month, and the United States was no closer to winning the war than it had been in the beginning.

The following excerpts explore the issue of war as it unfolds in *Slaughterhouse-Five*. They cover the development of Vonnegut as an antiwar writer; one character's escape from World War II through psychological time travel; the author's search for a literary structure that would suit the chaotic horror of war; and the philosophy that Vonnegut shapes through asking the question "Why do the innocent suffer?"

Chronology

1922

Kurt Vonnegut Jr. is born in Indianapolis, Indiana, on November 11. His parents, Kurt Vonnegut Sr. and Edith Lieber, are third-generation German Americans.

1936–1940

Vonnegut attends high school and writes and edits a student newspaper.

1940

Vonnegut enrolls in Cornell University, majoring in chemistry and editing *The Cornell Daily Sun*.

1942

The United States enters World War II.

1943

Vonnegut enlists in the US Army.

1944

Vonnegut's mother commits suicide on Mother's Day.

Vonnegut is captured by Germans during the Battle of the Bulge on December 19.

1945

In February, while Vonnegut is held in an underground meat locker in Dresden, Germany, Allied air forces bomb the city, destroying it. The number of civilians killed is estimated at 135,000 (a 2008 German commission revised the number to no more than 25,000).

In May he returns home and is awarded a Purple Heart.

The US bombs Hiroshima on August 6, killing 71,379 people.

Vonnegut enrolls at the University of Chicago and works as a news bureau reporter.

He marries Jean Marie Cox.

1947–1950
Vonnegut works in public relations for General Electric in Schenectady, New York.

1951
Vonnegut moves to Massachusetts to write full-time.

1952
His first novel, *Player Piano,* is published.

1954
He takes on teaching and writing jobs to support his wife and three children.

1957
Vonnegut's father dies.

1959
The Sirens of Titan is published.

1961
With the help of poet George Starbuck, Vonnegut's works are reissued.

1962
Mother Night is published.

1963
Cat's Cradle is published.

1965
God Bless You, Mr. Rosewater is published.

Starbuck hires Vonnegut to teach at the Iowa Writers' Workshop.

1967

Vonnegut goes to Germany to do research for *Slaughterhouse-Five*.

1969

Slaughterhouse-Five is published.

1972

A film adaptation of *Slaughterhouse-Five* is released.

1973

Breakfast of Champions is published.

1979

Vonnegut divorces Cox and marries photographer Jill Krementz.

1981

Vonnegut publishes *Palm Sunday: An Autobiographical Collage*.

1985

Vonnegut's novel *Galapagos* is published.

1987

Bluebeard is published.

1997

Timequake is published.

2000

Vonnegut is hired to teach advanced writing at Smith College in Massachusetts.

2005

Vonnegut appears in a documentary titled *The American Ruling Class*.

2006

Vonnegut gives his last face-to-face interview.

2007

Vonnegut is featured in a film, *Never Down*.

Vonnegut dies on April 11.

Michael Moore dedicates his film *Sicko* to Vonnegut.

Social Issues in Literature

CHAPTER 1

Background on Kurt Vonnegut

Vonnegut's Family and the Success of *Slaughterhouse-Five*

Peter J. Reed

Peter J. Reed, professor emeritus at the University of Minnesota, is the author of The Vonnegut Chronicles.

In this viewpoint, Reed recounts that Kurt Vonnegut's prosperous ancestors came to the United States from Germany in the nine- teenth century. After World War I his father (an architect), his mother, and their families suffered from anti-German sentiment and did what they could to suppress their own German culture. When Vonnegut returned from World War II, he attended gradu- ate school at the University of Chicago. While in school he worked as a journalist, and later he worked in public relations. He began writing fiction during this time. In 1965 his career blossomed, earlier works were republished, and he received a two-year appointment to the Writers' Workshop at the Univer- sity of Iowa. By the 1970s Vonnegut had gained attention from literary academic circles. He received honorary degrees and an appointment as a distinguished professor. His writing is known for its irreverent criticism of the social establishment and its nontraditional form. In Slaughterhouse-Five, *Reed believes, war is a metaphor for the human condition and the painful inevita- bility of death and the absence of meaning.*

Though Kurt Vonnegut had been a widely read short-story writer throughout the 1950s and though his novels had developed a cult following in the 1960s, it was in 1970, when his novel *Slaughterhouse-Five; or, The Children's Crusade* (1969) caught the mood of a country disillusioned with the Vietnam War, that he achieved widespread acclaim. Since then his ear-

Peter J. Reed, "Kurt Vonnegut," *American Novelists since World War II: Dictionary of Literary Biography*, ed. James R. Giles and Wanda H. Giles. Gale Research, 1995.

lier novels have been studied with increased attention, while his steady production has continued to keep his name before the public. Besides his popularity in the United States, Vonnegut's work has been widely translated, achieving particular success in Britain, Germany, and Russia. All fourteen of his novels remain in print, a remarkable feat considering that they cover a career of some forty-five years. The novels and short stories continue to be adapted for film, television, and theater. His nonfiction works—including *Wampeters, Foma and Granfallonns (Opinions)* (1974), *Palm Sunday: An Autobiographical Collage* (1981), and *Fates Worse Than Death: An Autobiographical Collage of the 1980s* (1991)—underline his role as an American literary icon and respected social observer, and he frequently is sought out for speeches, interviews, and commentary.

A Social Critic with a Background in Journalism

Vonnegut has come to be recognized as a thoughtful social critic who ponders the impact of technology, science, and social behavior. A skeptical observer with a light touch, he charms and amuses readers with his humor and irreverence while unflinchingly exposing the foibles of society. The technique in much of his work may be characterized as postmodern; rather than revering classical prose models, it instead uses choppy, vernacular sentences and deemphasizes traditional conventions of plot, theme, time, and character development. Like postmodern buildings, which may unite the architecture of disparate styles and eras, his novels combine comedy with pathos, fantasy with history, and didacticism with farce. Such forms as poetry, science fiction, satire, drama, graffiti, lyrics, drawings, and even recipes appear in the novels. They deconstruct the social myths on which society often thoughtlessly runs and repeatedly defamiliarize the commonplace daily world to make their audience reexamine its habits of thinking.

Vonnegut cuts quickly to the issue, actions are reported succinctly, and the prose is geared toward moving the story along and holding the reader's attention. His style, conspicuous for its short sentences and paragraphs, owes much to his background in journalism. As a satirist he acknowledges his debt to Voltaire and Jonathan Swift, while his brand of humor is influenced by Mark Twain and comedians such as Laurel and Hardy, W.C. Fields, and Bob and Ray. Vonnegut's enduring themes—social injustice, economic inequality, environmental exploitation, and militaristic barbarity—spring from his experiences growing up in the Depression [of the 1930s] and surviving World War II. Through his usually damaged, faltering antiheroes his stories search for what gives life meaning in a society bereft of cultural certainties.

Vonnegut's German Ancestry

Vonnegut was born in Indianapolis, Indiana, on 11 November 1922. His forebears came to the United States as part of the heavy wave of German immigration of the mid-nineteenth century, two of his great-grandfathers—Clemens Vonnegut Sr. and Peter Lieber—arriving in 1848. They both eventually found their way to Indianapolis, where Lieber bought into a brewery in the 1860s and with a combination of business acumen and political awareness made his fortune. By the end of the century he had retired in style to Germany, leaving his son, Albert, to run the brewery and to indulge his extravagant tastes. Meanwhile, Clemens Vonnegut's son Bernard had become an architect, as did in turn his son Kurt. They were cultured men who revered the arts, especially poetry and music.

Both families became well established professionally and socially and were joined on 22 November 1913 by the marriage of Kurt Vonnegut and Albert Lieber's daughter, Edith Sophia Lieber. From this marriage came three children: Bernard in 1914, Alice in 1917, and Kurt Jr. in 1922. As Vonnegut reflects in the introduction to *Slapstick, or, Lonesome No More!*

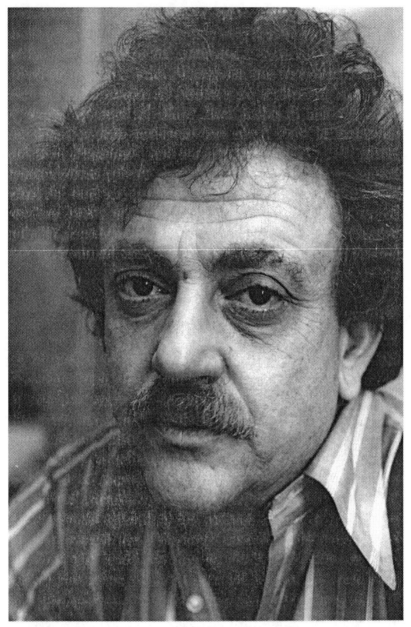

American author Kurt Vonnegut Jr. earned the praise of American antiwar activist with his 1969 novel Slaughterhouse-Five, or, The Children's Crusade. *Associated Press.*

(1976), the children were born into a large, prosperous family that offered the support of many close relatives and the security of a preserved cultural heritage, things for which he later yearned nostalgically.

Anti-German sentiment after World War I and the general erosion of distinctions of place and heritage in an increasingly mobile, homogenized America contributed to the cultural decline of German American society in Indianapolis. Financial blows also fell. Prohibition [when the manufacture and sale of alcohol was banned in the United States from 1920 to 1933] ended the Lieber income from brewing, and the Depression brought a halt to building and hence unemployment to Vonnegut's architect father. Looking back on those years Vonnegut has said that during the Depression his family never went hungry, and although they moved to a new, somewhat smaller house, designed by his father, their lifestyle was not crimped. But his father found no work for ten years and became increasingly withdrawn and tentative. The experience was something Vonnegut seems never to have forgotten, and his fiction abounds with characters who fall into self-doubt when they lose productive social roles. . . .

Vonnegut's Military Experience

In 1944 Vonnegut was sent to Europe and shortly thereafter was captured during the famous Battle of the Bulge of December 1944, becoming a prisoner of war in Dresden, Germany. He survived the firebombing of Dresden on the night of 13 February 1945 in an underground meat-storage cellar used as an air-raid shelter, emerging the next morning to find only smoking ruins. For the next several days he and other prisoners were employed pulling corpses from the debris and cremating them. These events became the basis of his best-known novel, *Slaughterhouse-Five*. In April 1945 Russian troops occupied Dresden, and he was liberated.

After a period in a military hospital in Europe, trying to rebuild his already lean frame after losing thirty-four pounds while a prisoner, he returned to Indianapolis with the Purple Heart. He married his high-school sweetheart, Jane Marie Cox, on 1 September 1945, and they moved to Chicago. There he pursued graduate work in anthropology at the University of Chicago while working for the Chicago News Bureau. . . .

Fact and Fiction

In 1947 Vonnegut moved to Schenectady, New York, to work as a public-relations writer for General Electric, where his brother, Bernard, already worked as a scientist. The job, the plant, the town, and the people he encountered there provided settings, characters, and situations for many of his stories. Initially, though, the job provided well-paid employment that enabled him to draw on both his journalistic experience and the scientific emphasis of his education. These elements combined when he began writing fiction. Many of his colleagues from the public-relations department at General Electric would describe how they aspired to become writers, but Vonnegut dedicated long hours after work and on weekends to his writing. The bombing of Dresden was the subject about which he felt compelled to write, but finding the form through which to approach it proved difficult. It was to be twenty years before he actually came to it. . . .

In 1951 Vonnegut moved to Provincetown, Massachusetts, and later to West Barnstable, living on Cape Cod for almost twenty years. During this time he and Jane had three children; Mark, Nannette, and Edith. In 1957 they adopted three of the four children orphaned when his sister died of cancer within forty-eight hours of her husband's death in a train crash. This bizarre and painful incident, compounding the impact of his mother's suicide and his own wartime experiences, appears to have contributed to his attitudes toward life and the strange and often brutal twists it can take. There are references to couples who die within hours of each other in several of his novels. . . .

The Pinnacle of His Career: *Slaughterhouse-Five*

At this point in his career Vonnegut's fortunes began to turn. The first printing of *God Bless You, Mr. Rosewater* (six thousand copies) in March 1965 was quickly followed by a second printing, of seven thousand copies, in May. The Dell paperback edition, published in April 1966, ran to 177,855 copies. Dell also reissued *Cat's Cradle* in September 1965, with 150,000 copies printed, and in 1966 *The Sirens of Titan*, with 201,703 copies. Avon came out with paperback printings of *Player Piano* and *Mother Night*. In addition to this mounting commercial success, in 1967 he received a Guggenheim Fellowship to travel to Dresden and gather material for the novel on that experience, which was to emerge as *Slaughterhouse-Five*. In the course of preparing the novel Vonnegut visited his old friend Bernard O'Hare, who had been a scout, then a prisoner, with him in Germany, and who was now an attorney in Pennsylvania, to see whether they could together uncover more specific recollections. It was then, as Vonnegut notes in the introduction to *Slaughterhouse-Five*, that Mary O'Hare objected to the conception of the story, which could have been turned into a movie starring John Wayne and Frank Sinatra. Vonnegut recalls, "She freed me to write about what infants we really were: 17, 18, 19, 20, 21. We were baby-faced, and as a prisoner of war I don't think I had to shave very often. I don't recall that was a problem."

Later Vonnegut sought to put the Dresden experience into perspective, claiming that it had less influence on his life than *Slaughterhouse-Five* would suggest. Perhaps it was easier for him to make such a disclaimer after writing about the experience. Perhaps, too, his characteristic modesty urged him to back away from something he might have felt was being sensationalized. Nevertheless, the importance of the event for his fiction, if not his life, seems undeniable, as apocryphal disasters, visions that embody the symbolism of Dresden, haunt novel after novel. His resistance to exaggerating the importance of a short-term event does reinforce the point, though, that earlier, less dramatic experiences influence his fiction just as significantly.

Despite Vonnegut's claim in the first chapter that the book is a failure, *Slaughterhouse-Five* succeeds remarkably well both in encompassing the personal trauma he experienced in Dresden and in emphasizing its universal human significance. To do so demanded an artistic innovation evolving from the form of the previous three novels that is most apparent in the unusual narrative perspective of the book. The novel is a first-person narration, although glancing at any page in the middle chapters may make it seem to be third-person omniscient. Vonnegut speaks as himself about his experiences and the writing of *Slaughterhouse-Five* not in a separate preface or introduction but in the first chapter. He returns in the tenth and final chapter. In between he declares himself periodically as someone present in the action of the novel by saying "that was me" or "I said that." . . .

War as a Metaphor for the Human Condition

If war serves as his metaphor for the larger human condition and apocalypse functions as its ultimate consequence, in Dresden, Vonnegut finds the quintessential embodiment of these perceptions. It becomes the keystone of all he has to say about human behavior or the nature of human existence. The combination of personal involvement, historical authenticity, and symbolic meaning invests the Dresden of *Slaughterhouse-Five* with an impact more profound than any of his previous world-ending catastrophes. *Slaughterhouse-Five* integrates the personal and the public to achieve a unique richness; it remains its author's most intensely cathartic novel but also carries perhaps his most compelling social message.

That *Slaughterhouse-Five* appeared at a time when antiwar feeling over Vietnam was increasing in America no doubt helped its sales. The first printing in March 1969 ran to ten thousand copies, the first Delta printing a year later was twenty-five thousand copies, and the first Dell edition of 1971 was seven hundred thousand copies. The 1972 Universal Pictures film adaptation, directed by George Roy Hill, also contributed to the popularity of both book and author. Rather suddenly, twenty years into his career as a writer, Vonnegut found himself famous, prosperous, and even something of a guru figure to the Woodstock generation. Simultaneously he was at last earning the acclaim of academics, led by Leslie A. Fiedler, Tony Tanner, and [Robert A.] Scholes, and of reviewers.

Social Issues at the Time of *Slaughterhouse-Five*'s Publication

With the success of *Slaughterhouse-Five* Vonnegut emerged from a following of largely young audiences to wider recognition. Much of the developing interest in him was not simply in his role as writer but as social observer and popular philosopher. Many of his views struck a sympathetic chord in this era, not just about the war but on such issues as overpopulation, ecology, civil rights, and consumer protection. This popularity grew even greater in the next few years. In January 1970 he flew into Biafra, a part of Nigeria fighting for independence, accompanying an aircraft load of medical and food supplies. His visit was scarcely over when Biafra fell. His moving account of the suffering of the Biafrans and of the beauty and strength of their family system was published in *McCall's* [magazine] and later included in [his book of essays]

Wampeters, Foma and Granfalloons, though these impressions emerge most profoundly in *Slapstick*. . . .

Personal Trauma and Successes

By 1971 Vonnegut had separated from his wife and moved to New York. The next year brought another personal trauma when his son Mark suffered the onset of schizophrenia while living in a commune in British Columbia. In 1975 Mark published his account of this episode, *The Eden Express*. Vonnegut meanwhile seemed uncertain about the direction of his work. In 1972 a television screenplay based on his fiction, *Between Time and Timbuktu*, was produced by National Educational Television, and the illustrated script was published that year with an introduction by Vonnegut. His popularity was by now at its height, and he had achieved more serious critical and scholarly recognition as well. Two critical quarterlies, *Summary* and *Critique*, ran special Vonnegut issues in 1971, and two books—*Kurt Vonnegut Jr.* (1972) by Peter J. Reed and *The Vonnegut Statement* (1973), edited by Jerome Klinkowitz and John Somer, emerged from academe. Vonnegut received honorary degrees from Indiana University in 1973 and from Hobart and William Smith College in 1974, an appointment as Distinguished Professor of English Prose by the City University of New York in the fall of 1973 (he left in February 1974), and election as vice-president of the National Institute of Arts and Letters in 1975.

Vonnegut's Despair About War at the End of His Life

Loree Rackstraw

Loree Rackstraw is a retired English professor. She taught at the University of Northern Iowa.

In the following selection, Rackstraw, a friend of Kurt Vonnegut's since their days together at the Iowa Writers' Workshop, recalls his life in his late seventies and early eighties when the United States was at war in Iraq and Afghanistan. By that time he had become an iconic antiwar writer; other activists dared suggest that his World War II novel Slaughterhouse-Five *be required reading for all US troops. According to Rackstraw, Vonnegut's war heroes were never noble, exceptionally courageous people but instead were ordinary, naïve, even somewhat clownish figures, like* Slaughterhouse-Five's *protagonist, Billy Pilgrim. Perhaps for that reason Vonnegut has never been regarded as significant by the literary establishment, a situation that did not make him bitter. Deeply disturbed about the Middle Eastern wars, he was planning an antiwar poster book and a collection of antiwar letters that had been rejected by the* New York Times. *These were published instead in a journal he called* In These Times. *He also used the Internet (despite not having used it before) to make his views known.*

Much more compatible with Kurt's hope for human potential was the ability to play and create things of beauty. So he was happy to help out with a benefit exhibition at a Northampton gallery to help raise funds for a skate park for kids. After his grandson Ezra and pals' love for skateboarding had been frustrated by local laws, he joined Nanny's [his daughter's] family in contributing a "new suite of four prints" to kick off the fund-raising.

Vonnegut's Outrage at Injustice

But such generosity is not to overlook Kurt's copious ability to express outrage at injustice, arrogance, and stupidity, particularly when it came to politicians, including testimony before government bodies in defense of social justice or the arts. In 2002, with his eightieth birthday some two months away, he spoke on the first anniversary of the 9/11 attacks at Saint Marks on the Bowery:

> The world will little note nor long remember what we say here.
>
> This is became we are powerless.
>
> Peace has no representatives in Washington, DC.
>
> Why not?
>
> Peace is not entertaining.

A day later, he faxed the following message to the editors of the *New York Times*:

> It may give us some comfort in these worrisome times to know that in all of history only one country has actually been crazy enough to detonate atomic weapons in the midst of civilian populations, turning unarmed men, women, and children into radioactive soot and bone meal. And that was a long, long time ago now. . . .

Kurt's response to life was not to elevate his characters above a recognition of pain by creating tragic figures like Odysseus or Hamlet to die heroically with noble courage and elegance (often taking a lot of others with them), but rather to invent clownish heroes like Billy Pilgrim to muddle clumsily through, sustained by music or silly jokes or moments of humble awe or fantasies of sexual bliss. The power of this human comedic trait is a gentle but sustaining one, and not so likely to result in worldwide wars or holocausts. That its literary expression seems beneath the dignity or wisdom of some literary pedants in famous universities or political leaders of powerful countries or religious institutions is perhaps worthy of circumspection. . . .

Finding a Venue for His Antiwar Message

Of course the year 2003 was darkened by the onset of the Iraqi war and the long-threatened "Shock and Awe" assault on Baghdad beginning that March, understandably a distinct influence on everyone's perceptions about then. Kurt was frustrated that the *Times* wasn't printing his editorial letters. And then came a lucky compensation: He began writing for a Chicago-based biweekly news magazine called *In These Times*. Editor Joel Bleifuss had interviewed Kurt for a two-page story critical of the [President George W.] Bush policy, which began his long-term relationship with the journal. It was founded in 1976 to "identify and clarify the struggles against corporate power now multiplying in American society." The journal's masthead soon listed Kurt's name as a senior editor, with its Web site quote by him: "If it weren't for *In These Times*, I'd be a man without a country."

Indeed, it just may have given Kurt a new reason to live to have this venue for his outrage and grief about what was happening to the country. His articles provided a vent for his despair about the corporate powers of institutions, from Enron and WorldCom to television and the government, running roughshod and without conscience over average fellow humans here and abroad. It was, I believe, the first time Kurt could fully articulate his growing insight about why these institutions had become so heartless in their treatment of American citizens. . . .

When his *In These Times* interview was first posted on the Web, it resulted in hundreds of online responses from gratified readers and soon expanded the journal's *online* accounts into what editor Bleifuss called "one of the most popular sites on the Internet." It actually *was* something of a digital miracle: born-again Luddite [someone who is against machines] Kurt Vonnegut's online Web posting dialog with readers! This phenomenon (it was well known Kurt did *not* use the Internet) occurred because he could reply immediately by fax to questions sent by fax to him from the magazines' host page by Bleifuss, who instantly put his replies online. Readers wrote increasingly thoughtful observations and questions in this popular "dialogue." Kurt eventually bundled the printed dialogue with spiral binding to distribute to friends. So even though he wasn't writing books any more, at least he could share his creative concerns in a different venue.

Ironically, the Internet made Kurt's ongoing communication more readily available worldwide, to institution heads as well as average readers, which resulted in even more requests for his words of support. One such was the International Peace Foundation, to whom Kurt faxed on February 8, 2003, the following:

> Those Americans determined to make war on Iraq, a tyranny already quite effectively neutered by the United Nations, and one which has never threatened us, intend to divert us and themselves from America's local and immediate problems, which are profoundly disturbing, with a truly thrilling TV show. . . .

Old Soldiers Against War on Iraq

As comparisons go, I found it an interesting twenty-first-century perspective, when the July 2003 issue of *Vanity Fair* spotlighted a dramatic full-page photograph of three aging literary icons: Kurt, Gore Vidal, and Norman Mailer, describing them as "The last three lions of the World War II novel . . . who are all veterans of that war." The article asserted they "have distinguished themselves this year by taking strong stands against America's latest war." . . .

Vonnegut visits a former air-raid shelter in Dresden, Germany, on October 7, 1998. Slaughterhouse-Five *is based on his experiences as a German prisoner of war during the Allied bombing of Dresden in World War II.* Associated Press.

It seemed as though Kurt trudged into the year 2004 on the edge of weariness—obviously grieved by the political situation in Iraq as well as by the unceasing exploitation of the planet and its life potential. And perhaps by his own aging. . . .

Then, on January 20, 2004, George W. Bush, now a full-fledged war president and having been named "Man of the Year" by *Time* magazine, presented his upbeat State of the Union address to the nation. That speech inspired an urgent message from "Kilgore Trout" [a recurring character in Vonnegut's fiction] in the form of an *In These Times* interview with Kurt Vonnegut, following a so-called "Orange Alert" [the US Homeland Security Advisory System code color for "high risk of terrorist attacks"]. This spoof was tagged "Economic terrorist attack expected at 8 p.m. EST" and published under the title "State of the Asylum" in the March issue (pp. 18–19). The "interview" allowed Kurt to inform Kilgore Trout that our commander in chief was in a "made-for-TV movie," which is now our form of government. He further insisted the president was "sincere" when "he gave a tax cut to the rich because they could make wiser use of it than the government ever could." It concluded with the grim appraisal that "the planet's immune system is trying to get rid of us with AIDS . . . but not even *it* can keep George W. Bush from getting elected to a second term."

Of course he was grimly right, but at least he had a forum.

Fifty-Ninth Anniversary of the Bombing of Dresden

On Valentine's Day came another copy in my mail of his 1945 freed prisoner-of-war letter assuring his family he was alive, its tone an embryonic hint of what would become the Vonnegut style. The gesture of resending this letter in 2004, the fifty-ninth anniversary of the Dresden firebombing, clearly reflected Kurt's increasingly cynical despair about Iraq and the grim reality that now, nearly sixty years later, nothing had really changed. Major historic sites, cultures, and human beings were being destroyed, ironically again by American bombs. It was as though he felt utterly bereft of any new words to express his disappointment with humanity, perhaps with life itself.

It's obvious to Vonnegut aficionados, and it bears repeating, that he was one of the most patriotic Americans I ever knew, especially coming as he did from the proud heritage of German immigrants who, in the nineteenth century, gratefully celebrated this country's freedoms and opportunities. He was especially proud his German great grandfathers had fought on the Northern side in the Civil War.

Given Kurt's own World War II combat in the homeland of his ancestors, and nearly being killed by bombs from his own countrymen as a war prisoner—well, it *does* suggest a certain aspect of life's paradox had left an impression on his young psyche. I'm often reminded of his statement in *Slaughterhouse-Five* when, on a return visit twenty-two years *after* the firebombing, he quotes his Dresden taxi driver: "I hope that we'll meet again in a world of peace and freedom in the taxi cab *if the accident will*" (p. 2, emphasis added).

The powerful role of accidents in Kurt Vonnegut's war experience (and life) had begun then, when, in his view, the fluke of weather had sent British and American bombers to Dresden, rather than to a previously scheduled target. Clearly, that irony shaped his fiction as well as his life and worldview. . . .

About a week later, the revelations of [the torture of Iraqi prisoners by US Army military personnel in] Abu Ghraib prison became headline news, adding to his challenge to offer what he called comforting stories: cheerful admonitions to engage in creative activities and acts of kindness. It was here that he repeated again what his son Mark had told him years before about life's purpose: "to help each other get through this thing, whatever it is."

Vonnegut on His Writing and Life

Kurt Vonnegut, as told to John Casey and Joe David Bellamy

Joe David Bellamy, who writes both fiction and nonfiction and has taught English at several colleges and universities, is the author of the novel Suzi Sinzinatti. *John Casey is a fiction writer, a creative writing teacher at the University of Virginia, and the author of* Spartina.

This viewpoint presents an interview with Kurt Vonnegut in which Casey and Bellamy describe him as a personality who fills a room—a famous yet unself-conscious innovator. The interview was first published in 1968 and was updated in 1973. Vonnegut discusses being labeled a "black humorist," one who writes graveyard humor. He distances himself from science fiction writers and confesses that he is derided because of being labeled one. Vonnegut talks about the form of his novel Slaughterhouse-Five, *calling it a thin book that even men might read. Long novels, he says, delay getting to the point. He also discusses the bombing of Dresden and how he lived with his experience for twenty years after the war before writing about it. Readers collaborate with the writer, he explains, and he, the author, is a character in some of his books.*

He is a huge, slouching, loose-jointed man with a really impressive mustache. He talks easily, this great wounded bear of a man, and when he laughs, he booms. He has a presence, like a politician, without being portly. He fills a room. He is moody, truculent one instant, laughing contagiously the next. Kurt Vonnegut, Jr., is perhaps the best-known, if the

John Casey and Joe David Bellamy, "Kurt Vonnegut, Jr," *The New Fiction: Interviews with Innovative American Writers*, ed. Joe David Bellamy. University of Illinois Press, 1974. Copyright © 1974 Joe David Bellamy. All rights reserved. Reproduced by permission.

least self-conscious, innovator among American contemporaries. Read by the millions, his novels *Player Piano*; *The Sirens of Titan*; *Mother Night*; *God Bless You, Mr. Rosewater*; *Cat's Cradle*; *Slaughterhouse-Five*; and *Breakfast of Champions*; plays *Happy Birthday, Wanda June* and *Between Time and Timbuktu*; and stories in *Welcome to the Monkey House* have made Vonnegut a cult figure and a cultural hero in his own time.

Parts of the following interview were conducted in the winter of 1968 during a visit by Vonnegut to the Iowa Writers Workshop, where he had taught from 1965 to 1967. For details of the visit, see *The Vonnegut Statement* by Jerome Klinkowitz and John Somer. The interview was expanded and updated in the summer of 1973 by additional questions, which were relayed to Vonnegut by telephone.

Being Labeled a Black Humorist

KURT VONNEGUT: I know you'll ask it.

JOE DAVID BELLAMY: Are you a black humorist . . . ?

VONNEGUT: You asked it.

In the Modern Library edition of *The Works of Freud*, you'll find a section on humor in which he talks about middle-European "gallows humor," and it so happens that what [author Bruce] Friedman calls "black humor" is very much like German-Austrian-Polish "gallows humor." In the face of plague and Napoleonic wars and such things, it's little people saying very wry, very funny things on the point of death. One of the examples Freud gives is a man about to be hanged, and the hangman says, "Do you have anything to say?" The condemned man replies, "Not at this time." . . .

Anyway, the label is useless except for the merchandisers. I don't think anybody is very happy about the category or depressed about being excluded from it. . . .

Being Categorized as a Science Fiction Writer

JOHN CASEY: And the science-fiction label . . . ?

VONNEGUT: If you allow yourself to be called a science-fiction writer, people will think of you as some lower type, someone out of the "mainstream"—great word, isn't it? The people in science fiction enjoy it—they know each other, have conventions, and have a hell of a lot of fun. But they are thought to be inferior writers, and generally are, I think—at least the ones who go to conventions.

When I started to write, I was living in Schenectady, working as a public relations man, surrounded by scientists and machinery. So I wrote my first book, *Player Piano*, about Schenectady, and it was published. I was classified as a science-fiction writer because I'd included machinery, and all I'd done was write about Schenectady in 1948! So I allowed this to go on. I thought it was an honor to be printed anywhere. And so it was, I suppose. But I would run into people who would downgrade me. I ran into Jason Epstein, a terribly powerful cultural commissar, at a cocktail party. When we were introduced, he thought a minute, then said, "Science fiction," turned, and walked off. He just had to place me, that's all. . . .

Writing Short Books That Men Will Read

CASEY: What about your novel *Slaughterhouse-Five*?

VONNEGUT: It's . . . it's very thin . . . about as long as *The Bobbsey Twins* [a series of children's novels published between 1904 and 1979]. This length has been considered a fault. *Ramparts* [a magazine that published the novel in segments] called to ask if they had received all the manuscript. I said, "Yeah, that's it." I'm satisfied. They're satisfied. They just wanted to make sure they had all the paper they were entitled to.

But I think this is what a novel should be right now. I'd like, for example, to write books that *men* can read. I know that men don't read, and that bothers me. I would like to be a member of my community, and men in our society do not customarily value the services of a writer. To get their attention I should write short novels.

The reason novels were so thick for so long was that people had so much time to kill. I do not furnish transportation for my characters; I do not move them from one room to another; I do not send them up the stairs; they do not get dressed in the mornings; they do not put the ignition key in the lock, and turn on the engine, and let it warm up and look at all the gauges, and put the car in reverse, and back out, and drive to the filling station, and ask the guy there about the weather. You can fill up a good-size book with this connective tissue. People would be satisfied, too. I've often thought of taking one of my thin books (because people won't pay much for one) and adding a sash weight [used in constructing windows] to it just to give someone the bulk he needs to pay seven or eight dollars for the thing, which is what I need to really eat and stuff. . . .

Writing About the Dresden Disaster

CASEY: What about your novel *Slaughterhouse-Five?*

VONNEGUT: It was written to treat a disaster. I was present in the greatest massacre in European history, which was the destruction of Dresden by fire-bombing. So I said, "Okay, you were there."

The American and British air forces together killed 135,000 people in two hours. This is a world's record. It's never been done faster, not in the battle of Britain or Hiroshima. (In order to qualify as a massacre you have to kill *real* fast). But I was there, and there was no news about it in the American papers, it was so embarrassing. I was there—so say something about it.

The way we survived—we were in the stockyards in the middle of Dresden. How does a firestorm work? Waves and waves of planes come over carrying high explosives which open roofs, make lots of kindling, and drive the firemen underground. Then they take hundreds of thousands of little incendiary bombs (the size had been reduced from a foot and a half to the size of a shotgun shell by the end of the war) and scatter them. Then more high explosives until all the little fires join up into one apocalyptic flame with tornadoes around the edges sucking more and more, feeding the inferno.

Dresden was a highly ornamented city, like Paris. There were no air-raid shelters, just ordinary cellars, because a raid was not expected and the war was almost over.

We got through it, the Americans there, because we were quartered in the stockyards where it was wide and open and there was a meat locker three stories beneath the surface, the only decent shelter in the city. So we went down into the meat locker, and when we came up again the city was gone and everybody was dead. We walked for miles before we saw anybody else: all organic things were consumed.

Anyway, I came home in 1945, started writing about it, and wrote about it, and *wrote about it*, and WROTE ABOUT IT. This thin book is about what it's like to write a book about a thing like that. I couldn't get much closer. I would head myself into my memory of it, the circuit breakers would kick out; I'd head in again, I'd back off. The book is a process of twenty years of this sort of living with Dresden and the aftermath. It's like Heinrich Böll's book, *Absent Without Leave*—stories about German soldiers with the war part missing. You see them leave and return, but there's this terrible hole in the middle. That is like my memory of Dresden; actually there's nothing there. It's a strange book. I'm pleased with it. . . .

One thing we used to talk about—when I was out in Iowa—was the limiting factor is the reader. No other art requires the audience to be a performer. You have to count on the reader's being a good performer, and you may write music which he absolutely can't perform—in which case it's a bust. . . .

Putting Himself in the Book

BELLAMY: One of the techniques that a lot of writers have been using—and you do it in *Breakfast of Champions*—is to put yourself in the book as yourself, as the self-conscious creator of the whole show. Do you think this is a more honest way of approaching fiction? How did you come to do it yourself in *Breakfast*? Of course you did it in *Slaughterhouse-Five*, too.

VONNEGUT: An inner urgency. I don't know. You probably get to a point where you can afford to do more self-indulgent things. I am at the point now . . . my publishers tell me I'm at the point where absolutely anything I write is going to sell extremely well, that it's going to sell phenomenally. That's not a dream—it's true. . . .

Writers Are Important but Unappreciated

CASEY: One last question. . . .

VONNEGUT: I'll give you a disturbing answer. People are programmed, just like computers with this tape feeding out. When I was teaching student writers, I suddenly realized in most cases what I was doing was reaching into the mouth, taking hold of the piece of tape, pulling gently to see if I could read what was printed on it.

There is this thing called the university, and everybody goes there now. And there are these things called teachers who make students read this book with good ideas or that book with good ideas until that's where we get our ideas. We don't think them; we read them in books.

I like Utopian talk, speculation about what our planet should be, anger about what our planet is.

I think writers are the most important members of society, not just potentially but actually. Good writers must have and stand by their own ideas.

I like everything there is about being a writer except the way my neighbors treat me. Because I honor them for what they are, and they really do find me irrelevant on Cape Cod. There's my state representative. I campaigned for him, and he got drunk one night and came over and said, "You know, I can't understand a word you write and neither can any of your neighbors . . . so why don't you change your style, so why not write something people will like?" He was just telling me for my own good. He was a former English major at Brown.

CASEY: Did he win?

VONNEGUT: He went crazy. He really went bughouse, finally.

Social Issues
in Literature

Slaughterhouse-Five and War

Facing the Cruelties of Civilization and Its Wars

James Lundquist

James Lundquist has written books on American literary figures, including Chester Himes, Jack London, and Sinclair Lewis.

In the following viewpoint, Lundquist explains that war in Slaughterhouse-Five *becomes a metaphor for all the ills of society. Literary critics have often looked down on Kurt Vonnegut's nontraditional narrative style. Innovations he employs in the novel include having his characters experience the past and present at once, removing the element of suspense; and making his protagonist, Billy Pilgrim, entirely passive, someone to which things happen. Vonnegut is also a character in the novel, a writer trying to come to terms with his horrific experiences during the World War II Allied bombing of Dresden. He jumps back and forth in time (as Billy does) in his attempt to find answers to his questions. Billy's illusions of time-traveling and the planet Tralfamadore are his way of handling the ever-present reality of war and death.*

"*It is my duty* to describe something beyond the imagination of mankind," the correspondent for the London *Times* began his dispatch in April 1945, after British troops marched into Belsen—the first Nazi prison camp to be exposed to world scrutiny—and discovered over forty thousand malnourished and dying prisoners and more than ten thousand corpses. The problem that Vonnegut faces in all of his novels is essentially the same as the one the correspondent had to face at Belsen—the increasing gap between the horrors of life in the twentieth century and our imaginative ability to comprehend their full actuality.

James Lundquist, *Kurt Vonnegut*. Frederick Ungar Publishing Co., 1977. Copyright © 1977 Frederick Ungar Publishing Co. All rights reserved. Reprinted with the permission of the publisher, The Continuum International Publishing Group.

Life's Pain, Exemplified by Dresden

For Vonnegut, the subject matter is not simply Nazi atrocity; it is many other things—runaway technology, inflated views of human destiny, amoral science, the distribution of wealth in America, the senselessness of war as continued experience, and insanity in Midland City [a fictional city based on Vonnegut's hometown, Indianapolis, that appears in several of his novels]—but the aesthetic problem remains the same, whether the scene is the crystallization of the oceans or the firebombing of Dresden: How to conceptualize and define the night terrors of an era so unreal, so unbelievable, that the very term *fiction* seems no longer to have any currency....

To many critics, Vonnegut's novels do read as if they are haphazard in structure and simplistic in thought. [Literary critic] Robert Scholes has tried to reply to all this by pointing out that "*Serious* critics have shown some reluctance to acknowledge that Vonnegut is among the great writers of his generation. He is ... both too funny and too intelligent for many, who confuse muddled earnestness with profundity." But the only effective reply is to take a close look at what is probably Vonnegut's most widely read novel and perhaps his best, *Slaughterhouse-Five*....

Experiencing Past and Future at Once

The time-tripping, both by Billy [the novel's protagonist] and the narrator, produces an effect somewhat like that achieved in the Tralfamadorian novel—to see many moments at once. The time-tripping also serves to eliminate suspense. (We know not only of Billy's assassination long before the novel ends, but also how the universe will end—the Tralfamadorians blow it up experimenting with a new fuel for their flying saucers.) And the conclusion Vonnegut comes to after examining the causes and effects of Dresden is that there indeed is no moral, only the *Poo-tee-weet* of the bird call that Billy hears when he discovers that the war in Europe is over and he wanders out onto the shady streets of springtime Dresden. . . .

Billy at first seems to be merely an entity to which things happen—he is lost behind the lines during the Battle of the Bulge, he and Roland Weary are captured by the Germans, he survives the fire-bombing of Dresden, he marries, he is the sole survivor of a plane crash, he hallucinates that he is kidnapped by the Tralfamadorians, he appears on crackpot talkshows, and he is finally gunned down in Chicago. But through the constant movement back and forth in time that constitutes Vonnegut's narrative, we see Billy becoming his history, existing all at once, as if he is an electron. And this gives the novel a structure that is, to directly state the analogy, atomic. Billy whirls around the central fact of Dresden, the planes of his orbits constantly intersecting, and where he has been, he will be. . . .

Trying to Come to Terms with Dresden

Slaughterhouse-Five is . . . as much a novel about writing novels as it is an account of Billy Pilgrim and Dresden. In relating the difficulty he had in dealing with Dresden, Vonnegut prefaces *Slaughterhouse-Five* with an account of his own pilgrimages through time as he tried to write about his Dresden experience. The opening section consists of jumps back and forth in the author's life—from his return to Dresden on a Guggenheim grant to his return home from the war two decades earlier, from a conversation on the telephone with his old war buddy [Bernard O'Hare] to the end of the war in a beet field on the Elbe [River] outside of Halle [a city in Germany], and then on to the Chicago City News Bureau, Schenectady and General Electric [places where Vonnegut worked after the war], visiting O'Hare in Pennsylvania, teaching writing at the University of Iowa, and then Dresden and the Guggenheim trip once more.

Aftermath of the Allied firebombing of Dresden, Germany, on February 13 and 14, 1945. Associated Press.

The concern is always with the problem of writing the book—how to represent imaginatively things that are unimaginable—but in detailing his frustrations, Vonnegut conceptualizes his own life the way he later does Billy's, in terms of Tralfamadorian time theory [the Tralfamadorians can perceive a fourth dimension, time]. The structure of the chapter about writing the novel consequently prefigures the structure of the novel itself.

In that opening section, Vonnegut outlines his essential difficulty by elaborating on the misconception with which he began work on the novel. He states that he thought the book would be easy to write—all he would have to do is to simply report what he had seen. But this does not work. Too many other things get in the way. Why was Dresden, a supposedly safe city, bombed? Why did the American and British governments cover up the facts about the raid? What does the Dresden attack imply about American and British civilization? And, more important, why must Vonnegut's life always lead up to and go back to what he saw when he emerged from the slaughterhouse meat locker and looked at the moonscape that was once perhaps the most beautiful city in Europe? . . .

Vonnegut's impulse is to begin with his own experience, not with characters or ideas, but the ideas soon get in the way.

Dresden as an Obsession

Two structural possibilities come to mind. The first is suggested in the song Vonnegut remembers as he thinks about how useless, yet how obsessive, the Dresden part of his memory has been:

My name is Yon Yonson,

I work in Wisconsin,

I work in a lumbermill there,

The people I meet when I walk down the street,

They say, "What's your name?"

And I say,

"My name is Yon Yonson,

I work in Wisconsin. . . ."

When people ask him what *he* is working on, Vonnegut says that for years he has been telling them the same thing—a book about Dresden. Like Yon Yonson, he seems doomed to repeat the answer endlessly. But the maddening song suggests something else—the tendency many people (perhaps all) have to return to a central point in their lives in reply to the question of identity ("What's your name?"). . .

The Devastation of War and the Innocence of Boy Soldiers

The search for an approach also takes Vonnegut through an investigation of other works of literature that deal with catastrophe and the attitudes that surround it. He mentions an account of the Children's Crusade [when thousands of Christian European children supposedly set out In 1212 to fight Muslims and capture Jerusalem] in a nineteenth-century book, *Extraordinary Popular Delusions and the Madness of Crowds*. This account is used to underscore the contrast he draws between the serious business of war and the naivete of Billy Pilgrim, Roland Weary, and most of the other soldiers he depicts. He mentions *Dresden, History, Stage and Gallery*, by Mary Endell (published 1908), and its account of how Dresden, with all of its beauty, has been attacked repeatedly.

He quotes some lines from [poet] Theodore Roethke's *Words for the Wind* to suggest both his own confusion and the sense he has that, simply by moving ahead and back in time, the meaning of Dresden was being sorted out:

I wake to sleep, and take my waking slow.

I feel my fate in what I cannot fear.

I learn by going where I have to go.

He mentions Erica Ostrovsky's *Céline and His Vision* [a critical work on a nineteenth-century writer and doctor] and recounts how death and time also obsessed the insomniac French writer after he was wounded in World War I. And then he mentions the story of the destruction of Sodom and Gomorrah in the Bible and how Lot's wife, because of her compulsive looking back at the burning cities when she was told not to, was turned into a pillar of salt.

All of these references either give Vonnegut ideas and material or else they relate to his own reaction to Dresden, but they do not quite offer him the approach he is after. This, as we have seen, he had to discover for himself. . . .

The Persistence of War

The change that comes over Billy is mainly a result of the way he is forced to look at many things—Weary's triangular-bladed knife with its brass-knuckle grip, the picture of a woman attempting sexual intercourse with a Shetland pony, the German corporal's boots (in which Billy sees a vision of Adam and Eve), his Cadillac El Dorado Coupe de Ville in the suburban shopping center parking lot outside his office, the spastic salesman who comes to the door trying to peddle phony magazine subscriptions, St. Elmo's fire [a bright glow] around the heads of the guards and his fellow prisoners, the cozy interior of the guards' railroad car, the clock on his gas stove an hour before the flying saucer comes to pick him up, the backward movie he watches on television while he is waiting for the Tralfamadorians, and so on. Through recapitulating imagery, Vonnegut suggests how the simultaneous relationship of everything Billy sees and experiences is slowly revealed and how Tralfamadorian time theory, instead of merely being a comic example of Vonnegut's fondness for science-fiction motifs, develops naturally and logically out of Billy's unconscious awareness of his own life.

Vonnegut's use of recapitulating [repeated] imagery can be seen on almost every page of the novel, but the backward movie will serve as one of the best examples of this technique. Billy suddenly sees a movie of World War II running backward in his head. The bombers suck the fire and the bombs back into their bellies, the bombs are shipped back to the factories and dismantled, and the dangerous contents are reduced to mineral form and returned to the ground. The fliers turn in their uniforms and become high-school kids. Hitler and everyone else turns into a baby and, as Vonnegut writes, "all humanity, without exception, conspired biologically to produce two perfect people named Adam and Eve. . . ." The reference to Adam and Eve recapitulates the vision Billy saw in the German corporal's boot years before; and the barking of the dog he hears outside his house recapitulates the barking Billy heard just before the corporal captured him. . . .

Tralfamadore as a Way to Live with Dresden

Billy's vision is handled in a deceptively ambiguous way, of course. The repetition of imagery together with the juxtaposition of disparate events in Billy's life suggests that his trip to Tralfamadore is an hallucination and that the prescription he winds up advocating is essentially the result of the associative powers of his mind. The substance of his trip to Tralfamadore may well be the consequence of reading a Kilgore Trout [a fictional author] novel, and the whole business of time travel and the simultaneous existence of events may well be simply another of the human illusions Vonnegut attacks so frequently in his earlier novels.

But the point for Billy is that the Tralfamadorians *are* real, that the years of his life are the only time there is, and he is going to live every moment over and over again. In addition, there is the pragmatic value of his vision—it enables him to deal with the horror of Dresden and to get around the question of "Why me?" that echoes through the novel. Are his lenses rose-colored or not? It perhaps depends on the reader's own willingness to look into the fourth dimension with him. *Slaughterhouse-Five*, at any rate, gives us a glimpse of what that dimension might be like, and shows us at the very least how it is possible to gain a sense of purpose in life by doing what Billy Pilgrim does—he re-invents himself and his universe.

Time Travel as a Brief Escape from War Memories

William Rodney Allen

William Rodney Allen is a professor of English at the Louisiana School for Math, Science, and the Arts. He has written books on Southern author Walker Percy and filmmakers the Coen brothers.

In the following selection, Allen relates that it took years for Kurt Vonnegut to pry information about the World War II bombing of Dresden from officials, who insisted that facts about the event were classified. What he finally found out was that more people died during the Dresden firestorm than were killed by the atomic bombs in Hiroshima or Nagasaki, Japan. Vonnegut believed that he and his readers needed a new way to relate to institutionalized violence. In Slaughterhouse-Five *both the author and his protagonist travel back in time to remember the war. Constructing a new way to look at the topic, Vonnegut identifies the soldiers with the biblical Adam and the crucified Jesus Christ. The book is a "growing-up" novel: the awkward, naïve innocents, like Billy, are cast into experiences of violence and death. With the 1968 assassination of presidential candidate Senator Robert Kennedy, who campaigned to stop the Vietnam War, all hope seemed lost to Vonnegut. The endless killing brought the persistence of war and death into focus.*

The story of Dresden was a hard one for an American to tell for a simple reason: it was designed by the Allies to kill as many German civilians as possible, and it was staggeringly successful in achieving that aim. Because the government rebuffed his attempts shortly after the war to obtain in-

William Rodney Allen, *Understanding Kurt Vonnegut*. University of South Carolina Press, 1991. Copyright © 1991 University of South Carolina Press. All rights reserved. Reproduced by permission.

formation about the Dresden bombing, saying only that it was classified, it took Vonnegut years to realize the scale of the destruction of life on the night of February 13, 1945. What he eventually learned was that, by the most conservative estimates, 135,000 people died in the raid—far more than were killed by either of the atomic bombs the United States dropped later that year on Hiroshima and Nagasaki. Vonnegut was not killed himself in the attack by purest chance: he and a few other American POWs and their guards had available to them perhaps the only effective bomb shelter in the city, a meat locker two stories underground. They and only a handful of others survived the attack. . . .

A New Way to Convey a Continuing Horror

More than a conventional reminiscence of war, *Slaughterhouse-Five* is an attempt to describe a new mode of perception that radically alters traditional conceptions of time and morality.

Put most simply, what Vonnegut says about time in the novel is that it does not necessarily "point" only in one direction, from past to future. . . . If such a reversal is possible, then the famous description in *Slaughterhouse-Five* of a backwards movie (in which air force planes suck up bombs into themselves from the ground and fly backwards to their bases, where soldiers unload the bombs and ship them back to the factories to be disassembled) might be more than a wistful fantasy of a peaceful world. Of course, Vonnegut is less interested in new theories in physics than he is in his characters' confrontations with a world that makes no sense in terms of their old ways of seeing it. Hence, rather than beginning his story by quoting [German physicist Albert] Einstein, Vonnegut puts a particular person in a very particular situation: "Listen: Billy Pilgrim has come unstuck in time."

But that striking opening sentence comes not in chapter 1 but in chapter 2. Chapter 1 consists of Vonnegut speaking in his own voice about the difficulties of writing *Slaughterhouse-Five*. Beginning with his 1966 introduction to the reissued *Mother Night*, Vonnegut had begun to speak more openly about himself and about the autobiographical connections underlying his writing. In the opening and closing chapters of *Slaughterhouse-Five*, however, he takes that process much further....

Traveling Back in Memory

There are many reasons why such a traditional structure did not work for the novel Vonnegut wanted to write, but the principal one is that characters' lives, like those of real people, do not themselves proceed in one direction: in reality one does as much "backward" traveling in time through memory as "forward" traveling in anticipation of the future.... Vonnegut's own life, and Billy Pilgrim's, is characterized by an obsessive return to the past. Like Lot's wife in the Bible, mentioned at the end of chapter 1, Vonnegut could not help looking back, despite the danger of being turned metaphorically into a pillar of salt, into an emblem of the death that comes to those who cannot let go of the past....

A Christlike Figure

Paradoxically, in creating this cosmic, nonlinear narrative Vonnegut uses fragments of all sorts of traditional narrative forms, much as a bird might use twigs, bits of string, and its own feathers to construct a nest, something very different than the sum of its parts. As [scholar] Richard Giannone observes, "Graffiti, war memos, anecdotes, jokes, songs—light operatic and liturgical—raw statistics, assorted tableaux, flash before the reader's eye." The most important linear narrative ... is the Judeo-Christian Bible, which is itself a central motif in *Slaughterhouse-Five*. There time proceeds from the creation to man's fall to the birth, crucifixion, and resurrection of Christ to the end of time with the Second Coming....

That Vonnegut was conscious of doing so—that he found the Christian, linear vision of time no longer adequate—is apparent by his remarks in the novel on a book by [fictional author] Kilgore Trout called *The Gospel from Outer Space*. According to Trout, the traditional Gospels are flawed because they seem to suggest that the moral lesson one should learn from Jesus' crucifixion is: *"Before you kill somebody, make absolutely sure he isn't well connected."* In Trout's revised version of the story, rather than being the Son of God, "Jesus really *was* a nobody, and a pain in the neck to a lot of people with better connections than he had. He still got to say all the lovely, and puzzling things he said in the other Gospels." Yet when this nobody is crucified, the heavens open up with thunder and lightning, and God announces that he *"will punish horribly anybody who torments a bum who has no connections"*. In the course of the novel it becomes clear that the weak, hapless, clownishly dressed Billy Pilgrim is precisely this "bum who has no connections"—that he is in effect a sort of new Christ. Such observations as the fact that Billy lay "self-crucified" on a brace in his German POW [prisoner of war] boxcar, or that Billy "resembled the Christ of the carol" that Vonnegut takes as the novel's epigraph ("The cattle are lowing, / The baby awakes. / But the little Lord Jesus / No crying he makes") make clear that this identification of Billy as a Christ-figure is Vonnegut's conscious intention.

Like Christ, Billy brings a new message to the world, although it is a very different one from his predecessor's. And like Jesus he is an innocent who accepts his death, at the hands of an enemy who reviles and misunderstands him, as an opportunity to teach mankind the proper response to mortality. Both Billy and Jesus teach that one should face death calmly, because death is not the end. In the Christian vision the self after death proceeds forward in time eternally, either in heaven or hell; for Billy, however, "after" death the soul proceeds backward in time, back into life. As Billy learns from the Tralfamadorians,

When a person dies he only *appears* to die. He is still very much alive in the past, so it is very silly for people to cry at his funeral. All moments, past, present, and future, always have existed, always will exist. . . .

World War II as Climax

Once he [the reader] finishes the novel—after a few hours, perhaps in one sitting—the reader can visualize all of Billy's moments stretched out before him like the Rocky Mountains; further, he can see the author's life in the same way, all the way from World War II to the assassination of Robert Kennedy in 1968, when Vonnegut was composing the last pages of *Slaughterhouse-Five*.

Yet while the novel boldly attempts to do away with traditional chronological narration on one level, it still gives the reader a story that builds toward the bombing of Dresden, which is recounted in greatest detail late in the book. . . . One can easily follow the traditional *Bildungsroman* [growing-up novel] of Billy's life. Born in 1922, like his creator, he endured a childhood marked by intense fears—of drowning when his father subjected him to the "sink or swim method," of falling into the Grand Canyon on a family trip, of the total darkness when the guides extinguished the lights in Carlsbad Caverns. These early images have great relevance for Billy's fear and ineptitude in the war and afterward. His refusal to try to swim and consequent passive sinking to the bottom of the pool is a symbolic wish to return to the safety of the womb. Billy falls constantly in the novel—into ditches, from boxcars, from the sky in a plane crash—despite his intense fear of falling epitomized by his Grand Canyon experience. Finally, the darkness in Carlsbad Caverns prefigures that in the meat locker two stories underground in Dresden—the most important symbolic womb into which Billy retreats for safety. One of the many ironies of the book is that such a passive person should be one of the few to survive the destruction of the city. As Vonnegut says simply of his hero, "He was unenthusiastic about living."

The Unprepared Soldier

After this shaky childhood Billy attends college for only a few weeks before going off to war as an unarmed chaplain's assistant. In no time he is captured, along with a hapless tank gunner named Roland Weary, in the Battle of the Bulge, the last great German counteroffensive of the war. Freezing in inadequate clothing, hungry, frightened out of his wits, Billy becomes "unstuck in time" for the first time, finding himself living moments out of his past or his future. Weary dies in transit to the POW camp of gangrene of the feet, which he had claimed was caused when the time-tripping Billy abstractedly stepped on him. Before he dies, Weary tells his story to [fellow POW] Paul Lazzaro, who vows to avenge Weary's death by tracking Billy down after the war and killing him. Lazzaro is an emblem of the fact that a soldier can never really escape his war experiences—that they will always "track him down," even years later. In the POW camp the dispirited group of Americans is greeted by some hale and hearty Englishmen who have been there most of the war, growing healthy on good Red Cross food (sent by mistake in excessive amounts), exercise, and English optimism. They are the opposite of Billy, the fatalistic, disheveled weakling who simply drifts from one disaster to the next in helpless resignation. After a falling out with the Englishmen over personal hygiene and philosophical attitudes, the Americans are sent to Dresden, a supposedly "open" city [one that the Germans had surrendered and that should therefore not be bombed], where they soon have their rendezvous with the most significant day in the city's history, February 13, 1945. . . .

Wars Are Never Over

The cracks in the American dream show through Billy's apparently successful postwar life. [His wife] Valencia is a parody of consumerism, since she constantly consumes candy bars while making empty promises to lose weight in order to please

Billy sexually. Billy's son appears to be headed for jail as a teen-ager before he joins the Green Berets and goes off to fight in Vietnam. On his way to the office Billy stops at a traffic light in a burned-out ghetto area and drives away when a black man tries to talk with him. Vonnegut was obviously responding to the incredible social tensions of the late 1960s, which saw the burning of major portions of several American cities in race riots, the assassinations of [President] John F. Kennedy, [civil rights leader] Martin Luther King, Jr., and Robert Kennedy, and the seemingly endless acceleration of the war in Vietnam. A major reason *Slaughterhouse-Five* had the enormous impact it did was because it was published at the height of the conflict in Vietnam, and so delivered its antiwar message to a most receptive audience. In a book of powerful passages, there is no more powerful one than this at the end of the novel, in Vonnegut's autobiographical chapter 10: "Robert Kennedy, whose summer home is eight miles from the home I live in all year round, was shot two nights ago. He died last night." One of Robert Kennedy's promises in his presidential campaign was to stop the war, and when he died that hope seemed to die with him. For Vonnegut, and for Billy, it must have seemed that Dresden was happening all over again in Vietnam. . . .

Slaughterhouse-Five is built on the paradox that it appears to offer acceptance and even indifference as responses to the horrors of the twentieth century, when in fact it is a moving lament over those horrors—a piercing wail of grief over the millions of dead in World War II. Emblematic of this paradox is a short phrase from the novel that has become probably the best-known and most often repeated by his readers of any in Vonnegut's work: "So it goes." . . .

War and Death Are Inevitable

Every time someone dies in the novel—from [old army officer] Wild Bob to Valencia to Billy Pilgrim himself to Robert

Kennedy—Vonnegut repeats "So it goes." Once this pattern is established, Vonnegut has fun with it, as when he has Billy pick up a bottle of flat champagne after his daughter's wedding: "The champagne was dead. So it goes" (63). Thus the phrase finally embodies all the essential attitudes toward death in the novel—acceptance, sorrow, humor, outrage. If at times "So it goes" reads like a resigned "Let it be," it more often comes through as the reverse: "Let it be *different*—let all these dead live!" So Vonnegut does let them live, in effect, by positioning the Tralfamadorian idea that they are always alive in their pasts.

Despite its mask of Tralfamadorian indifference *Slaughterhouse-Five* conveys at times an almost childlike sense of shock that the world is such a violent place. Children form an important motif in the book, which is subtitled "The Children's Crusade." Vonnegut had chosen that ironic phrase as a way to reassure Mary O'Hare, [his war buddy] Bernard's wife, that he was not going to portray war as a glamorous affair fought by "Frank Sinatra and John Wayne or some of those other glamorous war loving, dirty old men." . . .

But *Slaughterhouse-Five* does not stop with the pathos of innocent children being killed. It refuses to be a self-satisfied antiwar book like, say, *Johnny Got His Gun*. While conveying a sense of outrage, horror, regret, and even despair over the insanity of war, Vonnegut does not think that stopping war is a realistic possibility or that, if it were, this would end the pain of the human condition. In chapter 1, when talking about his Dresden project to a movie producer, Vonnegut had gotten the response, "'Why don't you write an anti-*glacier* book instead?' What he meant, of course, was that there would always be wars, that they were as easy to stop as glaciers. I believe that, too." Even more significant is Vonnegut's admission that "if wars didn't keep coming like glaciers, there would still be plain old death." Finally, while Vonnegut accepts war and death as inevitable, he refuses to endorse the sentimentalized, childlike attitude of acceptance of the inevitable epitomized in the prayer hanging on Billy's office wall and inside a locket on a chain hanging around Montana Wildhack's neck: "God grant me the serenity to accept the things I cannot change, courage to change the things I can, and wisdom always to tell the difference." As Vonnegut observes, "Among the things Billy Pilgrim could not change were the past, the present, and the future." Dresden has happened, is happening, and will always happen.

Billy's Time Travel Is Not Science Fictional but Psychological

Arnold Edelstein

Arnold Edelstein is a literature scholar.

In this viewpoint, Edelstein argues that Kurt Vonnegut intends his protagonist Billy Pilgrim's so-called time travel as purely psychological rather than as an episode of science fiction. For example, Edelstein points out, Vonnegut repeatedly uses "he says" when he explains Billy's impressions of Tralfamadore. Billy's comments about time travel reveal that Tralfamadore has its roots in the events of his life on earth. His journeys into the past, in which war is dominant, only show that any person relives the past in the present. Billy's war experiences are actually meaningless, as is his decline into old age. Tralfamadore is an escape from the anguish with which he can no longer cope. Vonnegut's repeated references to Eden, Adam, and Eve, Edelstein explains, are meant to underscore Billy's false innocence and unrealistic happiness.

There is overwhelming evidence throughout *Slaughterhouse-Five* that every element of Billy's "sci-fi fantasy" can be explained in realistic, psychological terms.

Hints that Billy's Time Travel Is Psychological Fantasy

Perhaps aware of the reader's temptation to identify the author with his central character after hearing the author speaking in his own voice in the first chapter, Vonnegut begins the

Arnold Edelstein, "*Slaughterhouse-Five*: Time Out of Joint," *College Literature*, vol.1, no. 2, Spring 1974. Reproduced by permission.

second chapter with a clear assertion of narrative distance. Billy "has seen his birth and death many times, *he says*, and pays random visits to all the events in between. *He says.* . . . He is in a constant state of stage fright, *he says* . . . ." Two pages later, Vonnegut repeats this emphasis.

> *He said*, too, that he had been kidnapped by a flying saucer in 1967. The saucer was from the planet Tralfamadore, *he said*. He was taken to Tralfamadore, where he was displayed naked in a zoo, *he said*.

Vonnegut maintains the narrative distance that is established here throughout the novel by a rather complex formal structure which distinguishes, sometimes not too clearly, between four levels of narration: *Vonnegut's present tense* (chapters one and ten); *Billy's present tense* (his trip to New York and its aftermath); *a novelistic past tense of historical fact* (the war experiences, Billy's eighteenth wedding anniversary, and the plane crash); and *Billy's travels in time and space*, which contain both historical events and the Tralfamadorian episodes (generally woven throughout the war experiences). Only the last level, the flash-forwards, raise any problems. Most of these problems vanish, however, when we reconstruct a chronological time-sequence from the bits and pieces that Vonnegut gives us. For then we discover that the flash-forwards are actually reinterpretations of Billy's past experience in the light of a time fantasy that takes twenty years to develop, but that achieves full form only a short while before he communicates it during his visit to New York City. . . .

In 1965 his mother, recuperating from pneumonia in a nursing home, had asked him, "How did I get so *old*"—associated with the war because Billy thumbs through [the nonfiction book] *The Execution of Private Slovik* a few minutes later in the waiting room. When he was sixteen, a man suffering horribly from gas had told him, "I knew it was going to be bad getting old. . . . I didn't know it was going to be *this* bad"—associated with the war because it is recalled while Billy is in bed next to Bertram Copeland Rumfoord, the official historian of the Air Force, and is discussing the [1945] bombing of Dresden. Finally, on one of the days that Billy falls asleep at the office, he notices the license plate of his Cadillac, dated 1967, and wonders: "Where have all the years gone?" His son a sergeant in Vietnam, his daughter married, his house empty, Billy has nothing to look forward to but old age and death—and nothing to look back to but Dresden. . . .

Soon after his release from the hospital, Billy, possibly suffering the after-effects of a broken skull, sneaks off to New York City to communicate his time theory and its source to the world. Before he can get on a talk show, however, he wanders into a bookstore that specializes in pornography and thumbs through two books by [fictional author] Kilgore Trout—including the one about being kidnapped by extraterrestrials that he had read years earlier in the veterans' hospital. He also sees a girly magazine with the headline, "What really became of Montana Wildhack" and part of a blue [pornographic] movie that Montana had made as a teenager. The fantasy is now complete. The clearest indication that Vonnegut means us to see it as fantasy is his use of the same phrases, with the pronouns made singular in the second instance, to describe the photographs of Montana in the girly magazine and the photograph of Montana's mother on her locket, which Billy says he sees in the zoo on Tralfamadore [where they are caged together]: "They were grainy things, soot and chalk. They could have been anybody." Significantly, the message on the other side of the locket is the same as the prayer on the wall of Billy's office: "God grant me the serenity to accept the things I cannot change, courage to change the things I can, and wisdom always to tell the difference." It is clear at this point that all the significant details of Billy's life on Tralfamadore have sources in Billy's life here on Earth.

Arnold Edelstein argues that, in Slaughterhouse-Five, *Billy Pilgrim's alien abduction and intergalactic travels are in fact psychological fantasies constructed to alleviate his painful war memories.* Friedrich Saurer/Alamy.

War Is Not Just Remembered but Relived

Significantly, however, the time-travel elements of his fantasy—those flash-forwards based on historical fact—bring Billy no peace at all. They cause that stage fright he feels at never knowing "what part of his life he is going to have to act in next." They are, then, an excellent metaphor for a man's inability to keep the horrible experiences of his past from invading the relative serenity of his present. They are more frightening in Vonnegut's version because the earlier experiences are not just remembered; they are *relived.* The space-travel to Tralfamadore and what Billy learns there about time provide him with a framework in which he can make peace with both the horrors of his past and the horrors of his impending old age, and in which his entire life has meaning—a framework that neither reality nor the time-travel elements alone could provide. Instead of a lost, little man whose life is empty and filled with horror, Billy becomes a saviour, "prescribing corrective lenses for Earthling souls." As a prophet of the Tralfamadorian "way," Billy can now foresee a life that has direction and significant meaning—and he can foresee a martyr's death that is completely antithetical to the painful meaninglessness of his mother in the nursing home. . . .

The Necessity of Billy's Withdrawal

If Billy were an actual person, not a literary character, we could say that his resigned "so it goes," the leit-motif [dominant, recurring theme] of the novel, is earned at a price terrible enough to be psychologically consistent with the horror of Billy's experiences. The only way he can live with his memories of the past and his fear of the future and find meaning in both is to withdraw from reality into a pleasant but neurotic fantasy. Vonnegut's restructuring of the chronological sequence prolongs our confusion about what is going on until the end of the novel and allows us to see in a single moment of insight—the scene in the bookstore—exactly what Dresden has done to Billy. This ending has a potentially enormous emotional impact. . . .

In short, Billy's fantasy provides him with a hard-won escape from the horrors of death—both the violent death of Dresden and the natural death that he faces in the future—and from the moral responsibility of having to do something about war, his meaningless existence, the generation gap, ghetto riots, cripples who work magazine rackets, and so on. . . .

Continually Brought Out of Seclusion by Harsh Reality

Billy Pilgrim's withdrawal from reality is not a random one. Its pattern is obscured by Vonnegut's restructuring of the chronological sequence but becomes obvious when we take the Tralfamadorians' advice and look at only the pleasant moments in Billy's life. Oddly, Billy's most pleasant moments include the potentially terrifying incidents in which he is dropped into a pool by his father, is crammed into a cattle car with other prisoners of war, is stripped and scalded in a delousing station, is carried through Dresden after the bombing, and then is kidnapped by creatures that resemble green machines and [is] displayed in a zoo. As we shall see, the pattern is almost the same in all of these incidents: completely passive Billy is placed in a situation that is pleasant because it provides all the necessities of life and precludes anxiety but then is jolted back into reality. . . .

The American soldiers, who have been herded about like children and who have survived by eating syrup, are saved from the fire-bombing because they are being kept deep in the basement of a concrete slaughterhouse. A few days later, Billy is sleeping in the back of a "coffin-shaped green wagon. . . . He was happy. He was warm. There was food in the wagon, and wine . . ." We are told that this ride was Billy's "happiest moment." Complete with Billy's own tears and blood dripping from the horse's mouth, Billy is delivered from the wagon-coffin-womb by two obstetricians. Once again, Billy is reborn from a womb-like, pleasant death (the obstetricians look at the suffering of the horse as they would have looked at Christ being taken down from the cross) not into paradise but into a life that is filled with the horrors of actual death.

If Billy's escape from the horrors of reality is ultimately unsuccessful in each of these actual incidents, the final escape—into the fantasy of the zoo on Tralfamadore—is completely successful. . . .

References to a Phony Innocence

The frequent references to Eden indicate that, on one level, we are meant to take Billy and Montana as another Adam and

Eve. Eden myths, however, frequently mask and attempt to dignify escapist, regressive fantasies of the kind we have been discussing here. Significantly, just before he is kidnapped, Billy is watching a war movie on television that moves backwards from the landing of a decimated squadron in England after a bombing raid. Billy sees bullets being sucked out of planes and bombs returning from the ground into the bellies of the planes. Finally, in Billy's imagination, "everybody turned into a baby, and all humanity, without exception, conspired biologically, to produce two perfect people named Adam and Eve." This backwards movie may be one of Vonnegut's gems in the novel but it also indicates the function of the Eden imagery and its relation to the womb imagery. In the long run, Eden and the womb seem identical—places of retreat beyond which Billy cannot regress.

Billy Pilgrim, Vonnegut's everyman-schlemiel [unlucky person]-hero, reacts to the horrors of the world around him by withdrawing totally from reality. Billy is not merely an ostrich who hides his head in the pleasant moments of his past rather than facing the difficulties of the present and the future; but one who crawls back into the egg itself. It remains to be seen how Kurt Vonnegut—at least the Kurt Vonnegut of the first and last chapters—views this defensive behavior.

Kindness in the Face of Cruelty

Rachel McCoppin

Rachel McCoppin, a professor of communication at the University of Minnesota, Crookston, has published articles on a variety of subjects, including existentialism and American literature and culture.

Despite his antiwar messages, this selection points out that Kurt Vonnegut suspects that trying to stop wars is futile. McCoppin argues that he presents altruism—being kind—as a way of confronting and psychologically surviving war: people must not lose their sense of responsibility even in times of conflict. The many interviews with Vonnegut reveal his antiwar position, especially in his comments on the Vietnam War, which was being waged when Slaughterhouse-Five *was published. The central part of his philosophy is that even though ultimately life is meaningless, humans have choices and must confront life's misery by being kind to others. His protagonist, Billy, is a peaceable, innocent man who shows his compassion even during the killing and hatred of World War II. In the novel, McCoppin argues, Vonnegut affirms his belief in the social function of literature.*

World War II is a central component in many of Kurt Vonnegut's novels; he uses the topic of war to advocate altruism. As stated in *Slaughterhouse-Five* (1969), Vonnegut understands that it is pointless to write an antiwar book because wars are "as easy to stop as glaciers," yet, arguably, many of his novels still impart an antiwar message. . . .

Vonnegut's revolt against war . . . is for the benefit of the community of mankind. His form of revolt in these novels is

Rachel McCoppin, "God Damn It, You've Got to Be Kind: War and Altruism in the Works of Kurt Vonnegut," *New Critical Essays on Kurt Vonnegut*, ed. David Simmons. Palgrave Macmillan, 2009. Copyright © 2009 Palgrave Macmillan. All rights reserved. Reproduced by permission.

to have his characters embrace altruism. Through altruism in a time of war, his characters arguably attain self-actualization.

Personal Responsibility in Times of War

As Vonnegut stated in *Conversations with Kurt Vonnegut* (1988), there are two recurring themes throughout his works: "The first is Be Kind; the second is God doesn't care if you are or not," and in *Mother Night* (1961) Vonnegut introduces a third message: "We are what we pretend to be, so we must be careful what we pretend to be." Vonnegut repeatedly stresses the importance of personal responsibility in a time of war. . . .

In *Slaughterhouse-Five* Billy Pilgrim travels through time in order to see his own personal accountability; though he believed he was detached from the war, he experiences a moment that finally makes him cry when he realizes that he was responsible for the mistreatment of horses after the bombing of Dresden. . . .

Though it is not entirely certain that Vonnegut draws from his own life experiences for his novels, it seems likely. In 1944 Vonnegut was a prisoner of war in Dresden where he witnessed the slaughter of "135,000 civilian inhabitants—the largest massacre in European history. Vonnegut and his fellow prisoners were drafted as corpse-miners, taking the dead Germans from their shelters and stacking them in funeral pyres across the ravaged city" (*Vonnegut in America*). Indeed, it is accepted critical knowledge that Vonnegut frequently mentions Dresden in his novels.

Moreover, in many personal interviews, Vonnegut's beliefs on war are revealed. When speaking about Vietnam, he speaks honestly, condemning both society and the government: "Our 45,000 white crosses in Vietnam were the children of lower class families. . . . War was hell for them, and . . . highly paid executives are coming back saying, 'Yes, it's a wonderful business.'"

Vonnegut undoubtedly looks keenly at the sad and horrific side of existence, but he still holds onto the belief that mankind can choose to treat others with kindness:

> Any sadness I feel now grows out of frustration, because I think there is so much we can do.... I just know that there are plenty of people who are in terrible trouble and can't get out. And I'm so impatient with those who think it's easy for people to get out of trouble; I think there are some people who really need a lot of help.

Vonnegut makes it clear that he believes life is a series of constant choices, but he consistently states that the most important choice is to treat others with dignity....

Vonnegut's *Slaughterhouse-Five* begins with a chapter that is in part autobiographical about the author's true-life experience of surviving the bombing of Dresden. Vonnegut states that he understands fully that to write this "antiwar" novel will not put a stop to war: "there would always be wars ... they were as easy to stop as glaciers." So, knowing this, why does Vonnegut write this novel? ...

Accepting Responsibility

Vonnegut knows that *Slaughterhouse-Five* will be unlikely to instigate much social or political change, yet the novel does its best to promote the idea that we are responsible for our actions and that a greater acknowledgment of this culpability may influence the future for the better. When Mary O'Hare accuses Vonnegut of writing a novel that will popularize war, the traditional purpose of war novels is criticized: "'You'll pretend you were men instead of babies.... And war will just look wonderful, so we'll have a lot more of them. And they'll be fought by babies like the babies upstairs.' ... She didn't want her babies or anybody else's babies killed in wars." In order to address these accusations, Vonnegut states that his novel will be antiwar, recognizing the human cost of violence in its subtitle: "The Children's Crusade."

Slaughterhouse-Five appears bleak in nature: "It is so short and jumbled and jangled ... because there is nothing intelligent to say about a massacre. Everybody is supposed to be dead, to never say anything or want anything ever again." Yet, it offers hope, but this sense of hope is only brought about by the protagonist Billy Pilgrim, an individual who doubts popular opinion, thinks independently, and accepts personal responsibility in an otherwise desperate, indifferent world.

The Peaceable Billy

Billy Pilgrim is depicted as extremely different from the other soldiers in the novel. He is not in the war to fight; we are told that he is a "valet to a preacher [and] bore no arms." Billy seems to be against violence throughout the war; in fact, the absurdity of Billy's appearance and actions makes the people who care about the "honorable cause" of war, like Roland Weary, appear absurd. Perhaps most importantly, Billy is depicted as different because he is a time traveler. Aliens, called the Tralfamadorians, teach Billy how to time travel, and this ability serves to show the reader Billy's unique way of looking at life—choosing to focus, mostly, on the positive moments of life rather than the negative ones: "That's one thing Earthlings might learn to do, if they tried hard enough: Ignore the awful times, and concentrate on the good ones."

Billy's conscious concern for others makes him stand out, as is evident by the strange way he dresses. As mentioned earlier, Billy's attire makes some laugh in the midst of war. Eight Dresden soldiers, who are apprehensive about having the hundred American prisoners see them in their dilapidated condition, see Billy and laugh. Billy brings out the fact that both opposing sides in the war are composed of individual human beings: "Their terror evaporated. There was nothing to be afraid of. Here were more crippled human beings, more fools like themselves."

When Billy is captured, he serves to reveal that war is often only about prejudice. The Germans who capture Billy and the soldier he is with are farmers; they are "sick of war," wounded multiple times and sent continuously back to fight. Staring into the corporal's golden boots, Billy thinks of Adam and Eve, how they were "naked . . . so innocent, so vulnerable. . . . Billy Pilgrim loved them." He looks up into the face of another one of his captors and discovers that it is the face of a fifteen year old boy; he sees it as an angel's face: "the boy was as beautiful as Eve." There is no hatred here; even at the moment of his capture by the supposed "enemy," he is able to see them as worthy individuals. Billy is the main character of this antiwar novel because he chooses to see differently.

Later in the novel, Billy is the sole survivor in an airplane crash. When Billy's son, now a soldier, shows up at his hospital bed, Billy realizes the never-ending nature of war: "he was decorated with a Purple Heart and a Silver Star and a Bronze Star with two clusters . . . and he was a leader of men. . . . Billy Pilgrim closed his eyes again."

Throughout the novel, Billy commits many altruistic acts. When he is working in the syrup factory in Dresden, he chooses to hand Edgar Derby, the man condemned to die, a spoonful of vitamin-enriched syrup, though it was illegal to do so, because Billy knows that Derby is as malnourished as he is: "A moment passed, and then Derby burst into tears." Billy is also quite altruistic in his desire to teach the people of the world what he has learned from his experiences with the Tralfamadorians:

> The cockles of Billy's heart . . . were glowing coals. What made them so hot was Billy's belief that he was going to comfort so many people with the truth about time. . . . So many of those souls were lost and wretched, Billy believed, because they could not see as well as his little green friends on Tralfamadore.

Kindness in the Face of Atrocity

After all he has experienced, Billy wants to help others. He wants to show others how to manage in this hard world, and he believes teaching others about the Tralfamadorian philosophy will help people to cope. It appears that Vonnegut sums up his view of the novel's function with this quote: "If what Billy Pilgrim learned from the Tralfamadorians is true, that we will all live forever, no matter how dead we sometimes seem to be, I am not overjoyed. Still—if I am going to spend eternity visiting this moment and that, I'm grateful that so many of those moments are nice." Vonnegut speaks out about the destruction and despair of this world, but he also offers hope through the ability of people to choose to view the positive moments in life.

Perhaps the most telling scene in the novel reveals Billy crying for the first time during his war experience while he is driving a horse-drawn wagon, searching for corpses after the bombing of Dresden: "He burst into tears" after seeing the condition that the two horses pulling the wagon were in: "he hadn't cried about anything else in the war." In many ways this scene is the thematic climax of the novel. It is possible to suggest that the horses represent innocence, serving as a metaphor for all the living beings that were used to the point of death because of the inhumanity of men during wartime. Billy at this moment feels his personal accountability for this incident. Throughout the entire war, he is a man who floats in and out of consciousness and realities; but at this one moment, Billy realizes his own blame. He feels that he could have cared for the horses more than he did. This scene imparts a message of the importance of personal responsibility in all situations. From this point onwards, Billy is no longer aloof; instead of continuing to be a victim of circumstance, he learns the importance of altruism from this one incident. To constantly strive to be kind in the face of such sadness forms a kind of salvation for Billy. . . .

Vonnegut states in the closing chapter of the novel that one of the nicest moments of his personal life is going back to Dresden with his old war buddy Bernard V. O'Hare, which is in itself a scene about seeking the good in a bad situation. In Dresden, he reads "key facts about the world," how 10,000 people die a day of starvation, 123,000 die for other reasons, and yet 324,000 new babies are born each day. By the year 2000 the population was predicted to be 7,000,000,000; he concludes melancholically by stating that "'I suppose they will all want dignity.'" . . .

The sociopolitical role that Vonnegut believes authors should fulfill is further exemplified in Vonnegut's affirmation of the Communist belief in the social function of literature. . . . *Slaughterhouse-Five* arguably fulfils this criterion, offering a message of pacifism in opposition to America's proclivity toward militarism.

The Moral Problem of Billy's Fantasies

Tony Tanner

Tony Tanner was a longtime professor of English and American literature at Cambridge University and was largely responsible for the introduction of American literature into the British curriculum.

Kurt Vonnegut has explained that Slaughterhouse-Five *took so long to write and is short and jumbled because "there is nothing intelligent to say about a massacre." In this viewpoint, Tanner contends that the novel is not just about the World War II bombing of Dresden but also about death in general.* Slaughterhouse-Five *is scattered with corpses and the rigidity of lifelessness. With the many dead in protagonist Billy Pilgrim's life, he finds comfort in the creed of the inhabitants of the planet Tralfamadore: that things, including wars, just exist—there is no reason for them, and there is no such thing as free will. The Tralfamadorians teach him that one cannot change the past, the present, or the future; so, Billy learns to accept atrocities. This means that he exchanges Western moral law and his conscience for passivity and acceptance. His new escapist ideas cannot keep him from weeping, however. The planet Tralfamadore unquestionably represents escapism, but escapism is sometimes necessary in the face of war and death.*

Here [in *Slaughterhouse-Five*] for the first time Vonnegut appears in one of his own novels, juxtaposing and merging the fantasies of his own life in a book which seems almost to summarize and conclude the sequence of his previous five novels. Slaughterhouse-Five was the actual address of the

Tony Tanner, *City of Words*. Harper and Row, 1971. Copyright © 1971 Harper and Row. All rights reserved. Reproduced by permission.

place where Vonnegut was working as a prisoner-of-war, and from which he emerged to witness the results of the Dresden air-raid. After seeing that, he tells us, he was sure that the destruction of Dresden would be the subject of his first novel. But he discovered that the spectacle of the Dresden fire-storm was somehow beyond language.

War Haunts the Soldier Continually

He describes how, over the years, he has tried to put a version together and make a novel, until now, at last, his famous Dresden war novel is finished, 'short and jumbled and jangled, Sam, because there is nothing intelligent to say about a massacre,' he adds apologetically to his publisher. But of course it is jumbled to very effective purpose. For it is not a novel simply about Dresden. It is a novel about a novelist who has been unable to erase the memory of his wartime experience and the Dresden fire-storm, even while he has been inventing stories and fantasies in his role as a writer since the end of that war. This book too will be a mixture of fact and invention ('All this happened, more or less'—so the book starts), for Vonnegut has created a character called Billy Pilgrim, whose progress entails not only undergoing the wartime experiences which Vonnegut remembers, but also getting involved in the fantasies which Vonnegut has invented. The result, among other things, is a moving meditation on the relationship between history and dreaming cast in an appropriately factual/fictional mode.

Reality Is Too Hard to Face

Summarizing the line of the story that Vonnegut tells, we can say that Billy Pilgrim is an innocent, sensitive man who encounters so much death and so much evidence of hostility to the human individual while he is in the army that he takes refuge in an intense fantasy life, which involves his being captured and sent to a remote planet (while in fact he is being transported by the Germans as a prisoner-of-war). He also comes 'unstuck in time' and present moments during the war may either give way to an intense re-experiencing of moments from the past or unexpected hallucinations of life in the future. Pilgrim ascribes this strange gift of being able to slip around in time to his experience on the planet which has given him an entirely new way of looking at time. We may take Vonnegut's word for it that the wartime scenes are factual, as near as can be attested to by a suffering participant. The source of Pilgrim's dreams and fantasies is more complex. The planet that kidnaps him is Tralfamadore, familiar from Vonnegut's second novel. At the same time it is suggested that the details of his voyage to Tralfamadore may well be based on details from his real experience subjected to fantastical metamorphosis. In his waking life Pilgrim is said to come from Ilium [a fictional town in New York] (see *Player Piano*); he later encounters the American Nazi propagandist Howard Campbell (see *Mother Night*); in a mental hospital he has long talks with [another character,] Eliot Rosewater, who introduces Pilgrim to the works of [fictitious author] Kilgore Trout, both familiar from Vonnegut's last novel [*God Bless You, Mr. Rosewater*]. Pilgrim is not only slipping backwards and forwards in time; he is also astray in Vonnegut's own fictions. Vonnegut himself enters his own novel from time to time. . . .

On the one hand the book is obsessed with death. This obsession is noticeable in Vonnegut's earlier works, but *Slaughterhouse-Five* is packed with corpses. It is the force which rigidifies life that holds Vonnegut's attention. He mentions Lot's wife [in the Bible], turned to a pillar of salt; this foreshadows the uncountable rigidified corpses which resulted from the Dresden air-raid. At one point a trainload of American prisoners is described as 'flowing' as it unloads like a river of human life. The last man of all on the train, a tramp, is dead. 'The hobo could not flow, could not plop. He wasn't liquid any more. He was stone. So it goes.' . . .

Tralfamadorians Believe No One Can Change Anything

This gives him an entirely new attitude to the significance and tragedies of those people who still live in an irreversible, linear-temporal sequence. From the Tralfamadorians he learns that all things from the beginning to the end of the universe exist in a sort of eternal present. They can look at time rather as one can scan a wide geographic panorama. Everything always *is*. 'There is no why.' This being the case everything that happens is exactly what has to happen. To use the Tralfamadorian image, we are all like bugs 'trapped in the amber of this moment'. The moment always exists; it is structured exactly as it had to be structured. For the Tralfamadorians the strangest thing they have encountered among Earthlings is the meaningless concept of 'free will'. Clearly this very lofty temporal perspective, like a heightened Oriental view of time, is, from our Occidental point of view, totally deterministic [dependent on fate]. More than that, it countenances a complete quietism [annihilation of the will] as well. A motto which Billy brings from his life into his fantasy, or vice versa, reads: 'God grant me the serenity to accept the things I cannot change, courage to change the things I can, and wisdom always to tell the difference.' In itself this is an open-ended programme. But immediately afterwards we read: 'Among the things Billy Pilgrim could not change were the past, the present, and the future.' Billy becomes completely quiescent, calmly accepting everything that happens as happening exactly as it ought to (including his own death). He abandons the worried ethical, tragical point of view of Western man and adopts a serene conscienceless passivity. If anything, he views the world aesthetically: every moment is a marvellous moment, and at times he beams at scenes in the war. Yet he does have breakdowns and is prone to fits of irrational weeping.

Everything Is All Right

Here I think is the crucial moral issue in the book. Billy Pilgrim is a professional optometrist. He spends his life on earth prescribing corrective lenses for people suffering from defects of vision. It is entirely in keeping with his calling, then, when he has learned to see time in an entirely new Tralfamadorian way, that he should try to correct the whole erroneous Western view of time, and explain to everyone the meaninglessness of individual death. Like most of Vonnegut's main characters he wants to communicate his new vision, and he does indeed manage to infiltrate himself into a radio programme to promulgate [spread] his message. He is, of course, regarded as mad. The point for us to ponder is, how are *we* to regard his new vision? According to the Tralfamadorians, ordinary human vision is something so narrow and restricted that to convey to themselves what it must be like they have to imagine a creature with a metal sphere round his head who looks down a long, thin pipe seeing only a tiny speck at the end. He cannot turn his head around and he is strapped to a flatcar on rails which goes in one direction. Billy Pilgrim's attempt to free people from that metal sphere, and teach his own widened and liberated vision may thus seem entirely desirable. But is the cost in conscience and concern for the individual life equally desirable? With his new vision, Billy does not protest about the Vietnam war, nor shudder about the effects of the bombing. The Tralfamadorians of his dreams advise him to 'concentrate on the happy moments of his life, and to ignore the unhappy ones—to stare only at pretty things as eternity failed to go by'. The Tralfamadorian response to life is 'guilt-free'. At one point Billy Pilgrim thinks of a marvellous epitaph which, Vonnegut adds, would do for him too. 'Everything was beautiful, and nothing hurt'. Later in life when a man called Rumfoord is trying to justify the bombing of Dresden to him, Billy quietly reassures him, "'It was all right . . . *Everything* is all right, and everybody has to do exactly what he does. I learned that on Tralfamadore.'" Yet he still weeps quietly to himself from time to time.

Fantasy Is a Legitimate Escape

Is this a culpable moral indifference? In later life we read that Billy was simply 'unenthusiastic' about living, while stoically enduring it, which may be a sign of the accidie [indifference] which settles on a man with an atrophied [withered] conscience. From one point of view, it is important that man should still be capable of feeling guilt, and not fall into the sleep which Germany and Europe slept as eternity failed to go by in the 'thirties. Can one afford to ignore the ugly moments in life by concentrating on the happy ones? On the other hand, can one afford *not* to? Perhaps the fact of the matter is that conscience simply cannot cope with events like the concentration camps and the Dresden air-raid, and the more general demonstration by the war of the utter valuelessness of human life. Even to try to begin to care adequately would lead to an instant and irrevocable collapse of consciousness. Billy Pilgrim, Everyman, needs his fantasies to offset such facts. . . .

While there is a kind of fiction which tries to awaken men to the horrors of reality . . . , it is clear to Vonnegut that there are fantasies, written or dreamed, which serve to drug men to reality. When the reality is the Dresden fire-storm, then arguably some drugging is essential.

Billy's Tralfamadorian perspective is not unlike that described in [Irish poet William Butler] Yeats's 'Lapis Lazuli'— 'gaiety transfiguring all that dread'—and it has obvious aesthetic appeal and consolation. At the same time, his sense of the futility of trying to change anything, of regarding history as a great lump of intractable amber from which one can only escape into the fourth dimension of dream and fantasy, was the attitude held by Howard Campbell during the rise of Nazi Germany. Vonnegut has, I think, total sympathy with such quietistic impulses. At the same time his whole work suggests that if man doesn't do something about the conditions and quality of human life on earth, no one and nothing else will. Fantasies of complete determinism, of being held helplessly in the amber of some eternally unexplained plot, justify complete passivity and a supine acceptance of the futility of all action. Given the overall impact of Vonnegut's work I think we are bound to feel that there is at least something equivocal [unclear] about Billy's habit of fantasy, even if his attitude is the most sympathetic one in the book. At one point Vonnegut announces: 'There are almost no characters in this story, and almost no dramatic confrontation, because most of the people in it are so sick and so much the listless playthings of enormous forces.' It is certainly hard to celebrate the value of the individual self against the background of war, in which the nightmare of being the victim of uncontrollable forces comes compellingly true. In such conditions it is difficult to be much of a constructive 'agent', and Billy Pilgrim doubtless has to dream to survive.

At the end of the novel, spring has come to the ruins of Dresden, and when Billy is released from prison the trees are in leaf. He finds himself in a street which is deserted except for one wagon. 'The wagon was green and coffin-shaped.' That composite image of generation and death summarizes all there is actually to see in the external world, as far as Vonnegut is concerned. The rest is fantasy, cat's cradles, lies. In this masterly novel, Vonnegut has put together both his war novel and reminders of the fantasies which made up his previous novels. The facts which defy explanation are brought into the same frame with fictions beyond verification. The point at which fact and fiction intersect is Vonnegut himself, the experiencing, dreaming man who wrote the book. He is a lying messenger, but he acts on the assumption that the telegrams must continue to be sent. Eliot Rosewater's cry to his psychiatrist, overheard by Billy Pilgrim, applies more particularly to the artist. "'I think you guys are going to have to come up with a lot of wonderful *new* lies, or people just aren't going to want to go on living.'"

A Nontraditional Way
of Conveying Chaos

Todd F. Davis

Todd F. Davis, professor of English at Pennsylvania State University at Altoona, is the author of more than ten books, including several collections of poetry.

In the following selection, Davis discusses the genesis of Kurt Vonnegut's unorthodox narrative style in Slaughterhouse-Five. *Vonnegut has said at times that Dresden and the war were not particularly important events in his life. At other times he has confessed that Dresden was such a horrific trauma that he could not remember it afterward, much less talk or write about it. He has described war as antithetical to normal behavior and to the ethics of peacetime. Davis relates that in the years following the war, Vonnegut tried to write about what was essentially chaos, to make sense of something that did not make sense. He was finally able to communicate his vision by discarding the traditional, romantic narrative patterns that cannot convey horror. His innovative scheme shows his disillusionment with old war romances as well as his distrust in the promise of science.*

For twenty-three years Vonnegut attempted to come to grips with the events he witnessed as a soldier in World War II. Like so many writers of his generation, Vonnegut experienced the cataclysmic affairs of war at the end of his youth, a formative time of philosophical contemplation that was exploded in the incendiary and violent deaths of 135,000 people living in Dresden. Undoubtedly the physical and spiritual impact of such a holocaust profoundly altered Vonnegut's

Todd F. Davis, *Kurt Vonnegut's Crusade*. State University of New York Press, 2006.

worldview, but, surprisingly, he has on occasion played down the importance of Dresden: "The importance of Dresden in my life has been considerably exaggerated because my book about it became a best seller. If the book hadn't been a best seller, it would seem like a very minor experience in my life." Some critics, [William Rodney] Allen among them, have actually taken Vonnegut's word on the matter, suggesting that Dresden "was no road-to-Damascus-like conversion" for Vonnegut. But to accept Vonnegut's assessment of Dresden's importance in his work and personal life requires the critic to ignore the assertions of contemporary psychology about the severe emotional stress war places on the individual, Vonnegut's own impressive body of work that deals directly or indirectly with Dresden and the theme of death by annihilation, and, quite simply, common sense. If we have learned anything by the end of the twentieth century, it is that war damages all life; the physical and spiritual destruction of war, the aftermath that festers like an open wound in the years that follow, cannot be shrugged off as inconsequential.

Making Sense of Chaos

A more honest appraisal of the matter of Dresden in the same interview when Vonnegut testifies to the fact that he has struggled with the memory of Dresden: "There was a complete blank where the bombing of Dresden took place, because I don't remember. And I looked up several of my war buddies and they didn't remember, either. They didn't want to talk about it. There was a complete forgetting of what it was like." Vonnegut represses the memory of Dresden and so much of World War II because of the terror it holds. The very actions that war demands of the individual are so antithetical to the normative behavior our culture praises in times of peace that many people cannot deal with what they have witnessed during combat action. To remember what has transpired is to

A Boeing B-17 Flying Fortress bomber, used extensively by Allied forces during World War II. British and American forces dropped nearly 3,000 tons of bombs on Dresden, Germany. Keystone/Staff/Getty Images.

relive what was unbearable in the first place, and, for Vonnegut, this means dredging the depths of his memory to behold once again the single greatest destruction of human life in modern military history. It is no wonder that Vonnegut blocked out any recollection of Dresden. As [scholar] Paul Fussell explains in *Wartime: Understanding and Behavior in the Second World War*, "When the war was over, for most of the participants there was nothing to be said. . . . [M]en of letters became silent." What does one say about the act of killing, whether ideologically justified or not? No ideology could place the events Vonnegut witnessed in a comprehensible pattern; what remained was merely chaos and silence, and, for over two decades, Vonnegut worked diligently to make sense out of what is most nonsensical, most absurd, in human behavior: war.

Therefore, *Slaughterhouse-Five* remains essentially a testament to one man's battle with the demons of war. Much, like [Ernest] Hemingway's Nick Adams or [Joseph] Heller's Yossarian, Vonnegut's [protagonist] Billy Pilgrim has been shaken to his very foundation by the bombs of war and longs to reconcile himself to the experience. But reconciliation is not to be his. Rather, Billy becomes unstuck in time, traveling to different moments in his life, as well as to the planet Tralfamadore where he discovers a coping strategy in the Tralfamadorian conception of time that enables him to work around the war, not through it. America can offer no grand narrative that makes sense of the atrocity Billy witnesses in Dresden, and the inhabitants of Tralfamadore make no attempt to fix meaning to any event, denying any notion of causality. Indeed, the novel itself appears emphatically and painstakingly to display the failure of traditional narratives to explain the violation of war. The structure of the novel—"somewhat in the telegraphic schizophrenic manner of tales of the planet Tralfamadore"—subverts the notion of causality in its own telling.

Loss of Faith

For Vonnegut then, Dresden represents his complete disillusionment with the grand narratives of American culture, especially the narrative of scientific progress in which Vonnegut had innocently placed his trust. After witnessing the awesome power of science in the service of humanity's hatred, Vonnegut essentially lost faith. . . .

Out of his lost faith, Vonnegut created his most formally post-modern [a movement that reconsiders modern assumptions about culture, history, and language] novel to date. The radical shift in form from any modernist conception of the novel results from Vonnegut's struggle to find a new paradigm [philosophical framework] for the Dresden experience. . . .

Time Shifts Keep Readers from Finding Meaning in War

The time shifts in *Slaughterhouse-Five* are exactly what prevent the writer and the reader from developing causes and effects, from creating meaning based on a metanarrative [a more complete plot]; there is a staunch refusal to try to explain how the bombing of Dresden could be justified. Moreover, the refusal to use chronological time represents the deconstruction [taking apart to expose biases and flaws] of one more grand narrative of western civilization; the idea behind chronological time as an organizing principle is to show the linear progression, the causes and the effects, of "history." Because Billy Pilgrim believes that this commitment to time as linear is the cause of humanity's woeful condition, he sets out, as any good optometrist would, to give Earthlings corrected vision. He writes in a letter to the newspaper:

> The most important thing I learned on Tralfamadore was that when a person dies he only appears to die. He is still very much alive in the past. . . . It is just an illusion we have here on Earth that one moment follows another one, like beads on a string, and that once a moment is gone it is gone forever. . . .

But does Billy's conception of time truly offer little more than the allusive façade of dreams, of science fiction? The answer to this question may be found in Vonnegut's own response to the war and in an examination of Billy's sanity. We must not forget that Vonnegut plays a crucial role in the first and last chapters of the novel and that Billy's response to Dresden does not represent Vonnegut's own response. While it is true that both Vonnegut and Billy tell their stories in order to cope with the darkness that threatens to engulf them, it remains a common mistake to conflate the two. [Scholar] Thomas Wymer argues convincingly that the lessons Billy learns from the Tralfamadorians about the nature of suffering and death in the universe do not embody Vonnegut's own convictions. Indeed, Vonnegut warns against the very kind of fatalism [a belief in fate] that the Tralfamadorians preach, consistently pointing out that the creatures who embrace such a philosophy are machines. Machines do not reflect the inner workings of humanity, and Vonnegut, of all people, would never suggest that humanity take its cues from any of science's great achievements, especially machines. In the fifth chapter Vonnegut makes it clear why Billy and Eliot Rosewater turn to the writing of [fictional author] Kilgore Trout to solve their crises: "They had both found life meaningless, partly because of what they had seen in war. . . . So they were trying to reinvent themselves and their universe. Science fiction was a big help." And science fiction is, indeed, what Billy uses to cope with . . . his schizophrenic condition. Science fiction, quite simply, offers Billy a chance to escape the confines of his grim and macabre existence. To come unstuck in time is to be free of any earthly shackle, and the conventions of slick science fiction can present no more cliché or unrealistic a fantasy life than the planet Tralfamadore, replete with a sultry Hollywood starlet in the form of Montana Wildhack. Time travel is Billy's therapy; his stories are his delusions.

Vonnegut Is Not a Fatalist

Conversely, Vonnegut uses writing as a form of therapy and social protest. Unlike Billy, Vonnegut never loses sight of the physical reality of war in the telling of his tale. Very early on Vonnegut admits that antiwar books are as effective as antiglacier books. The reality remains that there will always be war. And in the carnage of war, we will find the names of the victims and their stories, and out of humanity's violent refuse [waste] will come the survivors marked by the scars of living and their longing to forget what will forever haunt them. But Vonnegut, the optimist and the survivor, will not be daunted. He must write about Dresden; the ethics of human atrocity compel him to speak out against the insanity of war, to affirm the value of all life. In the first chapter, which echoes Benjamin Franklin's address to his son in *The Autobiography*, Vonnegut instructs his own sons against the practices of massacres:

> I have told my sons that they are not under any circumstances to take part in massacres, and that the news of massacres of enemies is not to fill them with satisfaction or glee.

> I have also told them not to work for companies which make massacre machinery, and to express contempt for people who think we need machinery like that.

Such words are not the words of a fatalist. After writing thousands and thousands of pages over two decades about World War II, Vonnegut refuses to make sense of Dresden and refuses to acquiesce to any notion of war; he throws away all he has written because as a "trafficker in climaxes and thrills and characterization and wonderful dialogue and suspense and confrontations," he cannot fit the reality of his experience into a conventional work of fiction. . . .

The Inability to Speak Coherently About War

Vonnegut's inability to speak cogently and coherently about Dresden represents the ethics of human atrocity. In *From the Kingdom of Memory*, [Holocaust survivor] Elie Wiesel suggests that the survivor speaks words, writes words, reluctantly, that writing for the survivor is not a profession, but a calling. In a moving passage, Wiesel explains, "I never intended to be a novelist. The only role I sought was that of witness. I believed that, having survived by chance; I was duty-bound to give meaning to my survival, to justify each moment of my life. I knew the story had to be told. Not to transmit an experience is to betray it." The ethics of human atrocity are created out of the need to testify to such experiences as the Holocaust and the fire-bombing of Dresden. As Wiesel claims, not to tell the story of survival is to betray it, and such a betrayal is as much a betrayal of self as it is a betrayal of those who perished. Therefore, if Vonnegut had proceeded to tell a conventional story about his time in Dresden, a story that reified the ideology of war, he would have committed an act of treason against all those long dead, their bones delivered into the earth, as well as an act of treason against all those who survive, their souls shattered. For this reason, Vonnegut's narrative is a failure by his own admission, a failure by modernist standards for the novel: "This one is a failure, and had to be, since it was written by a pillar of salt." To look back, to testify against the crimes of humanity, remains the only ethical choice for Vonnegut. In his testimony, he becomes nothing more than the salt of the earth, a pillar like Lot's wife. Vonnegut's choice to look beyond the pale, back toward the fruits of humanity's evil, gives to us a book of remarkable beauty. *Slaughterhouse-Five*, born out of one man's honest and human response to the carnage of our brutality, out of his rage against the sickness of war, endures as a paragon of post-modern morality.

Vonnegut's Denunciation of Tralfamadore

Robert Merrill and Peter A. Scholl

Robert Merrill is the editor of Critical Essays on Kurt Vonnegut *and has contributed to the essay collection* The Vonnegut Chronicles. *Peter Scholl is a professor of English at Luther College in Iowa.*

In the following selection, Merrill and Scholl argue that critics who mistakenly claim that Slaughterhouse-Five *is cynical and fatalistic distort Vonnegut's fundamental message. His novel of social protest can scarcely be thought of as teaching that humans cannot change. Nor can it be assumed, the authors state, that Vonnegut agrees with Billy's passivity. Furthermore, they contend, Tralfamadore is not a science fictional place but rather a figment of Billy's mind, psychologically contrived to help him face the dreadfulness of Dresden and death in general. By believing as the Tralfamadorians do that all moments exist at the same time, Billy can deny the reality of death and decide that "Everything was beautiful and nothing hurt." So Billy, unlike Vonnegut, does not attempt to change things but instead to rationalize them. Vonnegut's message is that neither he nor anyone fully human can truly accept death; according to Merrill and Scholl, he means to convey that a Tralfamadorian-type attitude actually led to the firebombing of Dresden and continues to cause wars and deaths.*

> I like Utopian talk, speculation about what our planet should be, anger about what our planet is.
>
> *Kurt Vonnegut, Jr.*

Robert Merrill and Peter A. Scholl, "Vonnegut's *Slaughterhouse-Five*: The Requirements of Chaos," *Studies in American Fiction*, vol. 6, no. 1, Spring 1978. Reproduced by permission.

In a recent issue of *SAF* [the journal *Studies in American Fiction*], [critic] Lynn Buck presents a view of Kurt Vonnegut which has become depressingly popular. Her very title, "Vonnegut's World of Comic Futility," suggests the drift of her discussion. Professor Buck speaks of Vonnegut's "deliberate mechanization of mankind," "the cynicism of the comical world he has created," and his "nihilistic [viewing existence as senseless] message." She concludes at one point that "to enter Vonnegut's world, one must abide by his rules, unencumbered by man-centered notions about the universe." There is some question, however, as to whether Buck is a reliable guide concerning the nature of these "rules." Her Vonnegut is a man who cautions against "man-centered notions about the universe," whereas the real Kurt Vonnegut once told a group of Bennington [College] graduates, "Military science is probably right about the contemptibility of man in the vastness of the universe. Still—I deny that contemptibility, and I beg you to deny it." Her Vonnegut is cynical and nihilistic, whereas the real Kurt Vonnegut recently said, "My longer-range schemes have to do with providing all Americans with artificial extended families of a thousand members or more. Only when we have overcome loneliness can we begin to share wealth and work more fairly. I honestly believe that we will have those families by-and-by, and I hope they will become international." In short, Buck's Vonnegut is a fiction. Vonnegut's readers know that he himself believes in certain kinds of fictions, "harmless untruths" which he calls *foma*. But Buck's version of Vonnegut is not harmless, for it leads her to distort the meaning of everything Vonnegut has written.

This reading of Vonnegut is all too representative. Repeatedly Vonnegut's critics have argued that his novels embody the cynical essence of Black Humor, a form so despairing as to contrast even with the relatively dark novels of a writer like Hemingway. The result has been a thorough misunderstanding of Vonnegut's vision in general and the meaning of his novels in particular. The distortion is most serious with Vonnegut's sixth novel, *Slaughterhouse-Five* (1969), for this is his one book that has a real claim to be taken seriously as a first-rate work of art. For this reason, it is crucial that the novel be interpreted properly. To do this, the notion that Vonnegut's world is one of comic futility must be abandoned. It must be seen that Vonnegut's advice to the Bennington graduates is embodied in his novels as well. . . .

Vonnegut's Novels as Agents of Change

It is safe to assume that novels of social protest are not written by cynics or nihilists. Surely protest implies the belief that man's faults are remediable. It is relevant, then, that Vonnegut's novels, early and late, were conceived in the spirit of social protest. . . .

Therefore, it is hard to believe that *Slaughterhouse-Five* is a novel that recommends "resigned acceptance" as the proper response to life's injustices. Tony Tanner is the only critic who has used the term "quietism" [passivity] in discussing *Slaughterhouse-Five*, but most of Vonnegut's critics seem intent on reading the book as if it *were* the work of a quietist. The problem concerns Vonnegut's "hero," Billy Pilgrim. *Slaughterhouse-Five* is about Pilgrim's response to the firebombing of Dresden. This response includes Billy's supposed space-travel to the planet Tralfamadore, where he makes the rather startling discovery about time that Winston Niles Rumfoord first made in Vonnegut's second novel, *The Sirens of Titan* (1959), "that everything that ever has been always will be, and everything that ever will be always has been." This proves immensely satisfying to Pilgrim, for it means "that when a person dies he only *appears* to die. He is still very much alive in the past, so it is very silly for people to cry at his funeral." Indeed, it is very silly for people to cry about anything, including Dresden. This is the "wisdom" Billy achieves in the course of Vonnegut's novel. It is, of course, the wisdom of quietism. If everything that ever has been always will be, and everything that ever will be always has been, nothing can be done to change the drift of human affairs. As the Tralfamadorians tell Billy Pilgrim, the notion of free will is a quaint Earthling illusion.

Misreadings of the Novel as Resigned Acceptance

What is more disturbing, Vonnegut's critics seem to think that he is saying the same thing. For [British author of *A Clockwork Orange*] Anthony Burgess, "*Slaughterhouse* is a kind of evasion—in a sense like J.M. Barrie's *Peter Pan*—in which we're being told to carry the horror of the Dresden bombing and everything it implies up to a level of fantasy. . . ." For [American critic] Charles Harris, "The main idea emerging from *Slaughterhouse-Five* seems to be that the proper response to life is one of resigned acceptance." For [American author] Alfred Kazin, "Vonnegut deprecates any attempt to see tragedy that day in Dresden. . . . He likes to say with arch fatalism, citing one horror after another, 'So it goes.'" For Tanner, "Vonnegut has . . . total sympathy with such quietistic impulses." And the same notion is found throughout *The Vonnegut Statement*, a book of original essays written and collected by Vonnegut's most loyal academic "fans."

This view of Vonnegut's book tends to contradict what he has said in published interviews and his earlier novels. But of course the work itself must be examined to determine whether or not *Slaughterhouse-Five* is a protest novel. Such a study should reveal Vonnegut's complex strategy for protesting such horrors as Dresden. . . .

The key to Vonnegut's strategy is his striking introduction of the Tralfamadorians into what he calls an antiwar novel. The fire-bombing of Dresden actually receives less emphasis than Billy Pilgrim's space and time travel, especially his visit with the Tralfamadorians. Vonnegut has played down the im-

Slaughterhouse-Five *contains allusions to several humanitarian tragedies that occurred after World War II, including the killing of hundreds of thousands of civilians in the Vietnam War.* Bettmann/Corbis.

mediate impact of the war in order to make "a powerful little statement about the kinds of social attitudes responsible for war and its atrocities," as Harris has remarked of *Mother Night*. By transporting his hero to Tralfamadore, Vonnegut is able to introduce the Tralfamadorian notions about time and death which inevitably call attention to more "human" theories. The status of the Tralfamadorians is therefore the most important issue in any discussion of *Slaughterhouse-Five*.

Tralfamadore as an Escape

It is the status of the Tralfamadorians themselves which is in question, not just their ideas. Vonnegut offers many hints that the Tralfamadorians do not exist. Just before he goes on a radio talk show to spread the Tralfamadorian gospel, Billy Pilgrim comes across several books by [fictional author] Kilgore Trout in a Forty-second Street porno shop:

> The titles were all new to him, or he thought they were. Now he opened one. . . . The name of the book was *The Big*

Board. He got a few paragraphs into it, and then realized that he *had* read it before—years ago, in the veterans' hospital. It was about an Earthling man and woman who were kidnapped by extra-terrestrials. They were put on display on a planet called Zircon-212.

It seems that the scenario of Billy's life in outer space is something less than original. Pilgrim gets his "idea" for Tralfamadore from Kilgore Trout. . . . Pilgrim may not literally be insane, but Vonnegut has undermined the reality of his experience on Tralfamadore. Indeed, the conclusion is irresistible that Pilgrim's space and time travel are modes of escape. Surely it is not coincidental that Billy first time-travels just as he is about to lie down and die during the Battle of the Bulge, nor that he begins to speak of his trip to Tralfamadore *after* his airplane crash in 1968. Faced with the sheer horror of life, epitomized by World War II and especially the fire-bombing of Dresden, Billy "escapes" to Tralfamadore.

If the very existence of Tralfamadore is in doubt, one might wonder about the ideas Billy Pilgrim encounters there. Billy takes great comfort in these ideas, but at first glance there would seem to be nothing very heartening in the Tralfamadorian philosophy. After all, the Tralfamadorians think of human beings as "bugs in amber." Like bugs, human beings are trapped in *structured* moments that have always existed and always will exist. For that matter, human beings are not really human: "Tralfamadorians, of course, say that every creature and plant in the universe is a machine." The Tralfamadorians would seem to be as jovial about life as the later [American author] Mark Twain.

But the Tralfamadorians have much to offer in the way of consolation. Most crucially, their theory of time denies the reality of death. Further, it allows man to pick and choose among the eternal moments of his existence. If everything that ever has been always will be, one can practice the Tralfamadorian creed and "ignore the awful times, and concentrate on the good ones." If one concentrates hard enough, he can have the same epitaph as Billy Pilgrim: "Everything was beautiful and nothing hurt." . . .

Billy Is Not a Heroic Changer but a Rationalizer

The irony here is that the Billy Pilgrims of this world *are* better off saying that everything is beautiful and nothing hurts, for they truly cannot change the past, the present, or the future. All they can do is survive. Tralfamadore is a fantasy, a desperate attempt to rationalize chaos, but one must sympathize with Billy's need to create Tralfamadore. After all, the need for supreme fictions is a very human trait. As one of Vonnegut's characters tells a psychiatrist, "I think you guys are going to have to come up with a lot of wonderful *new* lies, or people just aren't going to want to go on living." The need for such "lies" is almost universal in *Slaughterhouse-Five*. Most obviously, it lies behind Roland Weary's pathetic dramatization of himself and two companions as The Three Musketeers. It is most poignantly suggested in the religiosity of Billy's mother, who develops "a terrible hankering for a crucifix" even though she never joins a church and in fact has no real faith. Billy's mother finally does buy a crucifix from a Santa Fe gift shop, and Vonnegut's comment is crucial to much else in the book: "Like so many Americans, she was trying to construct a life that made sense from things she found in gift shops" Billy Pilgrim's "lie" is no less human and a good deal more "wonderful."

Billy Is Not Vonnegut

But finally Billy Pilgrim is not Everyman. One may sympathize with his attempt to make sense of things, but the fact remains that some men have greater resources than others. Indeed, some men are like Kurt Vonnegut. By intruding into his own tale, Vonnegut contrasts his personal position with that

95

of his protagonist. Billy Pilgrim preaches the Tralfamadorian theory of time until he becomes a latter-day Billy Graham [an American Christian evangelist]; Vonnegut looks with anguish at a clock he wants to go faster and remarks, "There was nothing I could do about it. As an Earthling, I had to believe whatever clocks said—and calendars." Billy Pilgrim sends his sons to Vietnam and the Green Berets [US Army special forces]; Vonnegut tells his sons "that they are not under any circumstances to take part in massacres, and that the news of massacres of enemies is not to fill them with satisfaction or glee." Vonnegut even tells his sons "not to work for companies which make massacre machinery, and to express contempt for people who think we need machinery like that." Billy Pilgrim says that God was right when He commanded Lot's wife not to look back upon [the biblical cities God destroyed because of their extravagant sin] Sodom and Gomorrah; Vonnegut writes *Slaughterhouse-Five* and so becomes [like Lot's wife] "a pillar of salt" himself. As [critic] Donald Greiner has said, "while Billy can come to terms with death and Dresden, Vonnegut cannot." Nor can anyone who would be fully human. . . .

Tralfamadorian Theories Cause Such Cruelties as Dresden

Finally there is a great difference between the quietistic notions of Tralfamadore and the injunction not to kill. The latter is a truly comforting "lie": it implies that human life is inherently valuable, and it suggests that men are capable of *choosing* whether or not they will destroy their fellow human beings. The consequences of accepting this idea are altogether agreeable. The consequences of believing in Tralfamadore and its theories are something else again. Vonnegut is careful to show that these consequences involve more than enabling Billy Pilgrim to achieve a sustaining serenity. They involve an indifference to moral problems which is the ultimate "cause" of events like Dresden. . . .

The scene involving Rumfoord and Billy Pilgrim is positioned at the end of *Slaughterhouse-Five* because it is the real climax to Vonnegut's complex protest novel. The object of satiric attack turns out to be a complacent response to the horrors of the age. The horror of Dresden is not just that it *could* happen here, in an enlightened twentieth century. The real horror is that events such as Dresden continue to occur and no one seems appalled. *Slaughterhouse-Five* is filled with allusions to such postwar disasters as Vietnam, the assassinations of [presidential hopeful] Bobby Kennedy and [civil rights leader] Martin Luther King, Jr., and the riots in American ghettos. Vonnegut stresses the kinship between these events and Dresden, most notably in the scene where Billy Pilgrim drives his Cadillac through a burned-down ghetto which reminds him "of some of the towns he had seen in the war." These are the problems Billy avoids in his life as Lions Club President, Tastee-Freeze entrepreneur, and Reagan supporter. These are the problems the [character of the] Marine major and Professor Rumfoord would see as "inevitable." But it is one thing to say that human problems are insoluble if one has visited Tralfamadore. It is quite another to support this view from a strictly Earthling perspective. Vonnegut's point is that insofar as men are guided by the likes of Professor Rumfoord, they act as if the Tralfamadorians were real and their deterministic assumptions valid. Yet Rumfoord's assertion that Dresden *had* to be is obviously false. The distinguishing feature of the raid on Dresden is that there was no strategic advantage to it whatsoever. . . . Man must judge his lies by their consequences, and the consequences are disastrous if people in power believe that Dresden was inevitable. In Vonnegut's view, the consequences are Vietnam, the ghettos, and a social order that seriously considers the election of Ronald Reagan as President of the United States.

Deromanticizing War

Stanley Schatt

Stanley Schatt has been an English professor at the University of Houston and has written on Kurt Vonnegut, Herman Melville, and Native American literature.

In this viewpoint, Schatt explains that Vonnegut creates three distinct voices in Slaughterhouse-Five: *that of the narrator, that of the protagonist Billy Pilgrim, and that of the author. As a character in the first chapter, Vonnegut describes his own attitude—that we must be kind and alleviate the suffering of others. It is the opposite of the ironic narrator's view that man has no free will to change anything, which corresponds with the view of the inhabitants of the planet Tralfamadore. Schatt asserts that even Billy has questions about that approach, though he preaches Tralfamadorian fatalism. The narrator does not appear to understand the extent of Billy's suffering because of the war and the desperation that drives him to escapism. The effect of the novel, according to Schatt, is to repudiate the romanticizing of war. It also denounces the government's attempt to cover up the atrocity of the World War II bombing of Dresden. In the novel's final chapter, Vonnegut confirms his view of the harsh realities of war and death.*

John Keats coined the term "negative capability" to describe the ability of the artist (in his case, the poet) to free himself from the confines of his own personality and ego and to adopt the identity of the person or persons he is writing about. While an artist who is able to annihilate his own personality when writing a novel has Keats's "negative capability," such annihilation is surely not within Vonnegut's capability in *Slaughterhouse-Five.* [Protagonist] Billy Pilgrim's reaction to the fire-bombing of Dresden is crucial to an understanding of Pilgrim's character. Because of the parallel in *Slaughterhouse-Five* between Vonnegut's experience in Dresden and that of Billy Pilgrim, Vonnegut creates a mask, a narrator who provides a certain distance between author and protagonist. . . .

This narrator has a Tralfamadorian philosophy of life which makes it painless for him to describe the fire-bombing of Dresden and Billy's suffering in a cold, detached, objective manner. Tralfamadorians, it should be remembered, are machines devoid of all human feelings of love and compassion. In the final chapter Vonnegut reappears and speculates on whether or not he can accept such a view of life.

Often, when an author uses a mask, its reliability may be questionable. In *Slaughterhouse-Five* Vonnegut is careful to distinguish his viewpoint from both Billy Pilgrim's and his narrator's. In the first chapter Vonnegut, speaking as himself, is not using a mask; and he explains that he loves the [biblical] wife of Lot for expressing her feelings of love and compassion by turning to look back at the inhabitants of Sodom and Gomorrah even though doing so means being transformed into a pillar of salt. What may be confusing is the fact that Vonnegut's view that man must try to ameliorate the suffering of his fellow man, or at least show some concern, is not shared consistently either by his narrator or by Billy Pilgrim. . . .

The Narrator Adopts Tralfamadorian Philosophy; Billy and Vonnegut Remain Skeptical

While Billy, like Vonnegut, is torn between a desire to forget Dresden and the pain this memory brings and an obsession about finding a way to reconcile the human suffering he observed there, the narrator pragmatically adopts the Tralfamadorian philosophy of "ignoring unpleasant times and concentrating on the good ones." He declares "so it goes" whenever he describes an unpleasant event such as the death of Billy's parents or the airplane crash that killed all the passengers except Billy. "So it goes" is a Tralfamadorian expression used by these robots to describe an unpleasant event which cannot be avoided since man and robot both live in a universe in which there is no such thing as free will.

While the novel's narrator reports that Billy turns away from a slight reminiscence of Dresden's fire-bombing, he does not appear to understand the motives behind such an action. Billy is not following the Tralfamadorian philosophy of indifference because, as a human filled with compassion, he cannot. Rather, his actions are a result of the equipoise [counterbalance] between his painful memories of Dresden and his almost intolerable fixation about the suffering he observed there. . . .

The major difficulty for the reader of *Slaughterhouse-Five* is that, while Vonnegut's narrator accepts the Tralfamadorian view of the universe wholeheartedly, Billy Pilgrim accepts this view intellectually but not emotionally. Emotionally, his view of the universe is much closer to Vonnegut's sentiments in the first chapter where the author speaks for himself: for Billy, like Vonnegut, cannot endure the sight of human suffering even though the Tralfamadorians tell him that there is nothing he can do about it. . . .

Repudiating the Romantic View of War

Slaughterhouse-Five is proof that Vonnegut kept his promise to write a war novel that does not glorify or glamorize killing. His novel does repudiate most of the stereotyped characters and patriotic bilge that has become standard movie fare. One of Billy's companions after the Battle of the Bulge is Roland Weary; he is stupid, fat, mean, and smells like bacon no matter how often he bathes; and he enjoys romanticizing the war until his daydreams blot out the reality of the frozen German landscape. While he is in reality unpopular, he imagines himself to be one of the three close war comrades who call themselves the "Three Musketeers." Vonnegut describes how Weary confronted Billy Pilgrim and "dilated upon the piety and heroism of 'The Three Musketeers,' portrayed, in the most glowing and impassioned hues, their virtue and magnanimity, the imperishable honor they acquired for themselves, and the great services they rendered to Christianity."

Weary's fantasy is counterpointed by Vonnegut's earlier description about an early Christian crusade—by the shocking reality of a children's crusade in which young boys are butchered or sold into slavery because of a war they cannot even comprehend. Vonnegut further deflates the idea that war is glorious and fun by describing a group of English prisoners of war who live in a self-supervised camp that they keep immaculate and well stocked with goods. They exercise regularly, keep themselves well bathed and groomed, and manage to preserve an atmosphere of normalcy. It is not surprising that the German commander adores them because "they were exactly what Englishmen ought to be. They made war look stylish and reasonable, and fun." The British prisoners are unaware that the soap and candles they use were made from "the fat of rendered Jews and gypsies and fairies and communists, and other enemies of the state." It is more than coincidental that they entertain Billy Pilgrim's group of bedraggled American prisoners by performing an adult version of Cinderella. They reinforce the German commander's justification for the war by transforming the ugly, horrifying realities of war into something beautiful and magical. But midnight tolls, and Billy once again sees the real picture of warfare when he goes outside to move his bowels. He finds all his fellow Americans terribly sick with diarrhea and suddenly becomes snagged to a barbwire fence.

Reworking Reality and Defending Atrocities

Vonnegut suggests that the United States Air Force tried to transform the Dresden fire-bombing from an atrocity to something almost heroic. While in a hospital recovering from an accident, Billy Pilgrim meets Bertram Copeland Rumfoord, a retired brigadier general in the Air Force Reserve and the official Air Force Historian. Rumfoord examines [British military historian] David Irving's *The Destruction of Dresden* because he is interested in the forewords by retired Lieutenant General Ira C. Eaker and by British Air Marshall Sir Robert Saundby. Eaker concludes his foreword by pointing out that, while he regrets that 135,000 people were killed in the fire-bombing of Dresden, he feels far worse about the five million Allies killed in the effort to destroy Nazism. As [critic] Donald J. Greiner has noted, Vonnegut despises Eaker's reasoning since the general apparently believed that the balancing of one atrocity with another by the other side neutralizes both and expiates all guilt.

Saundby's foreword, on the other hand, points out that the Dresden attack was not a military necessity; it was merely an unfortunate incident caused by circumstances. The men who approved the attack were not evil or cruel, but they may have been too remote from the reality of the war to understand the destruction such an attack would bring. Such a point of view is much closer to Vonnegut's reaction to the atrocity. Rumfoord reveals that the Dresden bombing has not heretofore been a part of the official Air Force history of World War II "for fear that a lot of bleeding hearts . . . might not think it was such a wonderful thing to do." Vonnegut finds such reasoning reprehensible.

The Point Is Death

While *Slaughterhouse-Five* is about the Dresden air attack and about World War II, its major focus is on death. Many deaths in the novel are ironic, especially that of unfortunate school teacher Edgar Derby who survives the Battle of the Bulge only to be shot for plundering a teapot from the ruins of the smoldering city. Vonnegut offers another view of death when he describes the Tralfamadorian view that all moments always have and always will exist and that death is just one moment in anyone's life. The Tralfamadorians enjoy the good moments and ignore the bad moments, but this solution is unsatisfactory to Vonnegut who believes that death is far too important to ignore.

Vonnegut's view of death becomes clear in the chapter of *Slaughterhouse-Five* in which he describes not his visit to Dresden in 1968 but Billy Pilgrim's efforts to dig up the bodies buried beneath the rubble of the fire-bombed city. When Billy is released from [German] captivity, Vonnegut describes the scene as follows:

> And somewhere in there was springtime. The corpse mines were closed down. The soldiers all left to fight the Russians. . . . And then one morning, they [the prisoners of war] got up to discover that the door was unlocked. World War Two in Europe was over.
>
> Billy and the rest wandered out onto the shady street. The trees were leafing out. There was nothing going on out there, no traffic of any kind. There was only one vehicle, an abandoned wagon drawn by two horses. The wagon was green and coffin shaped.
>
> Birds were talking.
>
> One bird said to Billy Pilgrim, "Poo-tee-weet?"

Billy's world is filled with both life and death. Though it is spring and the trees are leafing out, the coffin-shape of the abandoned wagon serves as a reminder of the death surrounding him. The last word in the novel is the bird's message to Billy Pilgrim, and it is the same message Eliot Rosewater received as [Vonnegut's earlier novel] *God Bless You, Mr. Rosewater* concluded. As [critic] Raymond Olderman has pointed out in *Beyond the Wasteland*, "Poo-tee-weet represents a 'cosmic cool,' a way of viewing life with the distance necessary to cope with the horrors that both Billy Pilgrim and Eliot Rosewater experience." It is not callousness or indifference but merely a defense mechanism that allows Vonnegut to smile through his tears and to continue to live and to write.

Slaughterhouse-Five concludes with Vonnegut himself describing among other things the latest casualty lists in Vietnam, the death of his father, the assassination of [presidential hopeful Senator] Robert Kennedy, the execution of kindly Edgar Derby, and the end of World War II. Though Vonnegut sees the Dresden fire-bombing in the context of the political assassinations and of the unpopular war [the Vietnam War] that overshadowed almost all other issues in the 1960's, he is able to smile through his tears and provide an affirmation of life. The message of *Slaughterhouse-Five* is the need for compassion: Malachi Constant ([protagonist of] *The Sirens of Titan*) and Billy Pilgrim both learn that the purpose of life, no matter whether there is free will or not, is to love whomever is around to be loved.

The War Novel: From Heroic Epic to Grim Reality

T.J. Matheson

T.J. Matheson, an English professor at the University of Saskatchewan, has published widely in scholarly journals on science fiction and on Kurt Vonnegut.

In the following viewpoint, Matheson documents Vonnegut's initial attempts to write about the Allied bombing of Dresden. These were abortive, Matheson argues, because Vonnegut attempted to use the usual war narrative structure, which tends toward romance. He learned, however, that such an approach trivializes the horrendous pain of war, a fact that his comrade O'Hare and O'Hare' wife immediately recognized when he told them about his planned novel. The older Vonnegut, who appears in the first chapter, comes to see that in his postwar adolescence, he had been a mere "trafficker" as a writer. Like other writers, he provided the public with pleasurable experiences. In the course of Slaughterhouse-Five, *Vonnegut points out that many people and groups attempt to cover up the truth—that all wars are cruel, war is chaos, and even when a war is over, moral order cannot be restored.*

Critics cannot agree on the meaning of Kurt Vonnegut's *Slaughterhouse-Five*. To Robert Merrill and Peter Scholl, the novel is best appreciated as a satire where "The object of satiric attack turns out to be a complacent response to the horrors of the age," in particular the Second World War. Though Dolores Gros-Louis agrees, seeing the novel as a plea for "active pacifism," Maurice O'Sullivan believes the solution

T.J. Matheson, "This Lousy Little Book: The Genesis and Development of Slaughterhouse-Five as Revealed in Chapter One," *Studies in the Novel*, vol. 16, no. 2, Summer 1984. Copyright © 1984 by University of North Texas. Reproduced by permission.

offered is more personal and argues that "Vonnegut offers art as the only potential form of transcendence" from such horrors. In contrast, Robert Uphaus claims that Vonnegut, dealing "with the all-encompassing problem of human imagination pitted against the forces of historical extinction," offers no clear solution to the problem, and Patrick Shaw, of all the critics the most pessimistic, concludes that "Vonnegut's theme [is] that history, sex, religion, and life in general are all waste products of a world which is itself universally inconsequential." . . .

A Moral Response to War

Upon inspection, it will be seen that the first chapter of *Slaughterhouse-Five* is of great importance in providing us with a means of tracing the author's evolving attitude both to the horrors of war and to the composition of his book as well. In this capacity, it outlines an artist's developing moral and aesthetic responses to a major aspect of the age in which he lived. Just as importantly, it also contains suggestions as to how *we* should respond intellectually and morally to war in particular and evil generally. For Vonnegut's theme is not as obscure as the structure of the work might imply. Indeed, there is every indication that his most fundamental concern is . . . simply with the problem of living in the midst of, and responding in a responsible manner to, evil as it is encountered in the modern world. . . .

Not the Romantic Epic Vonnegut Once Planned

Even obtuse readers could not fail to be alerted when the narrator remarks that "I would hate to tell you what this lousy little book cost me in anxiety and time." Since such a contemptuous reference to a novel [by] himself is not something we normally encounter, the reader can safely conclude that Vonnegut is speaking ironically and is not making a straightforward statement about the novel's literary worth, for if he genuinely did regard it as inferior—the usual meaning of the slang term "lousy"—he would surely not publish it in a form he found unsatisfactory. Obviously then, since the very appearance of the book is proof that Vonnegut regards it seriously, it is plain that he is not using the word "lousy" in the usual way. Since he does not appear to be speaking sarcastically, we are led to ask how the book might be "lousy" while not also being inferior. It is this question the remainder of Chapter One is concerned with answering.

Paradoxically, though here the narrator has just stated an apparent reluctance to outline the history of the novel's composition and his relationship to it, he proceeds to do just that and describes this history in considerable detail, in the process of which it becomes evident that we are also reading a history of the development of his character, as revealed through his evolving intellectual and artistic relationship not only to the book, but also to the central experience on which the book was based, the bombing of Dresden. As far as his actual character is concerned, Vonnegut wishes us to see the narrator (as a young man) as having been shallow, materialistic, and immature, and more than a little insensitive, for it is plain he initially regarded his war experiences as important primarily in terms of how they could advance his writing career. As a young man fresh from the Front, he naively "thought it would be easy for me to write about the destruction of Dresden, since all I would have to do would be to report what I had seen." With equal naiveté, he conceived his novel originally in epic terms suggestive of *Gone With the Wind*, "since the subject was so big," and thought it would virtually write itself and of its own accord emerge a "masterpiece" or at least make him "a lot of money." Epic war novels that make their authors rich likely have a mass appeal. To achieve this appeal, one suspects some sort of romantic sugarcoating of events—many of which are intrinsically grisly, horrid, and far from glamorous—must often take place, whereby they are rendered palatable to a mass audience. Evidently, the young author originally conceived his novel in such terms, probably as a romantic work that, if no true masterpiece, would nevertheless enjoy wide sales, in a word, a potboiler. However, "not many words" came from his mind, suggesting both that he soon learned it is not easy to write—about Dresden or anything else, for that matter—and also that on a deeper level, there was for all his immaturity a sense somewhere of moral and artistic responsibility to the events concerned. . . .

The Narrator's Oversimplified View of the Novel

The narrator's inability to recall where his old girlfriends live also attests to this imperfection of memory. But the most compelling evidence of this deficiency is seen in his attempt to stimulate his memory of the war by having a reunion with Bernard O'Hare, his old war buddy. Although ostensibly a sincere effort to face the past, it is plain that his approach to the proposed book is not yet well thought out. That he is taking neither the events of the war themselves nor the writing of the novel very seriously is suggested by the fact that he is drunk when he first contacts O'Hare. Childishness is also evident in the narrator's very diction, as seen when he explains to O'Hare that he would "'like some help remembering stuff.'"

It should come as no surprise, then, to learn that the novel as he originally conceived it was to have had a form, tone, and structure far different from that which *Slaughterhouse-Five* eventually assumed. By the narrator's own account, it appears to have been conceived along the lines of a conventional, popular war novel, full of action and suspense, easily understood by an unsophisticated reader and culminating in a conclusion wherein all issues appear to be resolved. It is plain, however, that the narrator will receive no help in this direction from the more mature O'Hare, a man too sensitive to the horrors of war ever to collaborate with a writer who would trivialize such experiences in fiction. Virtually alone among the prisoners of war, "O'Hare didn't have any souvenirs," possibly because war was so hideous to him that he refused to acquire any kind of booty or trophy that might become glamorous with the passage of time. Lest we miss this point, souvenir-hunting itself is portrayed as being either revoltingly ghoulish, in the case of the deranged [character] Paul Lazzaro who "had about a quart of diamonds and emeralds and rubies" taken "from dead people in the cellars of Dresden," or simply vulgar and garish, like the Englishman so impressed over his worthless and tawdry "plaster model of the Eiffel Tower." Notably, the young narrator also possessed a souvenir.

Understandably, O'Hare is "unenthusiastic" about the reunion and claims "he couldn't remember much," possibly because the memories are so painful, but more likely because he senses that the book the narrator is planning to write, as described, will fail to do justice to the truth. O'Hare has every reason to suspect the narrator of intending to exploit the war for his own purposes. There is something unmistakably unfeeling in the way the narrator alludes so enthusiastically to the death of "'poor old Edgar Derby,'" seeing it as an event important solely in terms of its irony and its resulting suitability as a possible climax for his novel, having more literary than human significance to him. This callous and cynical attitude to death suggests the narrator is not taking the war all that seriously; little genuine feeling is evident as he speaks. His very enthusiasm over the subject indicates he does not feel very deeply about it; one feels the sheer magnitude of the carnage ought to have a more sobering effect on a truly mature man. For that matter, the very importance he attaches to the novel's climax is significant when we recall that the word as a literary term usually heralds the appearance of the denouement, wherein all is resolved or unravelled. Clearly, the narrator himself intends to give the appearance in his novel of resolving issues that a more sensitive individual would see were beyond any such simplistic resolution, if they were resolvable at all. When asked "'where the climax should come'" O'Hare replies drily, "'That's your trade, not mine,'" his use of the word "trade" revealing his awareness of the extent to which the narrator's methods are, after all, more those of a mechanic or laborer than of a truly creative artist.

A War "Trafficker"

At this point, the narration shifts again to the novelist's present, from which vantage point the older narrator, seeing his initial approach to the novel's composition from a better perspective, recognizes himself as having been nothing more than a would-be "trafficker in climaxes and thrills and characterization and wonderful dialogue and suspense and confrontations. . . ." Vonnegut's use of the word "trafficker" is particularly apposite [appropriate], for in addition to the immediate suggestion of a dealer in illicit drugs, one of the meanings of the word "traffic" is "unlawful or improper trade." Since a trafficker, then, is one who engages in improper trade—precisely as the astute O'Hare recognized, one notes—a "trafficker" in literature must be a writer who presents for consumption something artistically improper, a kind of literary contraband or drug. It follows that any war novel designed as the narrator originally conceived his, to be merely thrilling and suspenseful, providing a merely pleasurable experience for the reader, is also a drug of sorts in that the reader's responses are being dulled as effectively as the body is by a chemical opiate. . . .

Military Denial and Silence

At the same time, there are many forces in society working to encourage such forgetfulness. As a civilian attempting to learn why Dresden was bombed, the narrator encounters resistance everywhere from military public relations [PR] men. Public relations itself is presented in *Slaughterhouse-Five* as a profession almost exclusively concerned with suppressing truth; importantly, the narrator after the war was in public relations. His boss in PR, we are told, joins the Dutch Reformed Church. This seemingly irrelevant bit of information, upon reflection, can be seen as ironically appropriate in light of that institution's Calvinistic emphasis on the total depravity of man. For that matter, the boss, through his profession and his attitude to war—an officer (in PR!) during the war, he sneers at the narrator for not having been an officer too—becomes himself convincing proof that the church's assumptions about human evil are correct.

A Dose of Reality About War

With his conventionally attired little girls, the narrator appears at the O'Hare house, expecting a comfortable evening of drink, good fellowship, and pleasant reminiscences. To his surprise Mary O'Hare, refusing to cater to his expectations, seats them on "two straight-backed chairs at a kitchen table with a white porcelain top. That table top was screaming with reflected light from a two-hundred watt bulb overhead," a far cry from the snug and cozy scene the narrator had sentimentally imagined, of "two leather chairs near a fire in a paneled room, where two soldiers could drink and talk." Unwilling to provide the narrator with an atmosphere conducive to nostalgia, Mary O'Hare presents them with "an operating room," the better to examine (and perhaps dissect) their memories honestly. O'Hare himself is unable to drink and as such cannot enter into the world of alcoholic sentimentality the narrator had anticipated. Not surprisingly, under such conditions neither man "could remember anything good," because in truth nothing good can ever be said of war. At this point Mary, angrily aware of the tendency in popular novels to find something of positive value in war, accuses the narrator of intending to do likewise and ignore the fact that wars are not fought by "'glamorous, war-loving, dirty old men'" but by babies, "foolish virgins . . . at the end of childhood." Mary recognizes that the very attempt to romanticize such horrors makes them palatable to a subsequent generation of "babies" who, ignorant of the hideous realities, rush headlong into new wars in a pathetic and misguided attempt to gain experience they mistakenly conclude their forefathers found meaningful.

At this point, the narrator attains a new level of understanding. To his credit, he both recognizes and sympathizes with what angered Mary and vows that he will write a book for which no parts could be played by Frank Sinatra or John Wayne, two actors we easily associate with typically unsophisticated and glamorous war movies. Furthermore, he promises to subtitle his book "The Children's Crusade" in acknowledgment of what Mary has taught him.

Once having seen this, the narrator's approach to his subject begins to change dramatically. In curiosity, he and O'Hare turn to an account of the original Children's Crusade [a legendary thirteenth-century war fought by European Christian children against the "infidel" Muslims of the Middle East], Charles Mackay's *Extraordinary Popular Delusions and the Madness of Crowds* (London, 1841), wherein much is made of the vast difference between the dispassionate historical record which reveals the [eleventh-to-thirteenth century religious] Crusades as a particularly distasteful chapter in human history—the Children's Crusade was nothing more than the result of an attempt by two cynical monks to sell homeless children into slavery in Africa—and the romantic account, which "*dilates upon their piety and heroism, and portrays, in her most glowing and impassioned hues, their virtue and magnanimity, the imperishable honor they acquired for themselves, and the great service they* [supposedly] *rendered to Christianity.*" Later that night he reads a history of Dresden left at his bedside by O'Hare which further sensitizes him to the fact that man's inhumanity to man is a recurring, if not also permanent, aspect of the human condition, be it manifested in the Children's Crusade, the destruction of Dresden by Frederick the Great [in 1760], or even the American Revolutionary War. Through this reading, the narrator comes to see that there are, broadly speaking, two approaches he can take to historical manifestations of evil, one straightforward, the other disingenuous [dishonest]: he can face all the facts squarely, letting them speak for themselves, or he can edit history by romanticizing or flatly ignoring events that are intrinsically sordid, unpleasant, or ugly, as he had originally intended to do. . . .

Moral Order Is Not Restored

Following his meeting with O'Hare, the narrator spent time at the Writers' Workshop at the University of Iowa, initially still at work on his "famous book about Dresden." But the O'Hares have had a lasting effect on his original plan for the novel; upon completion, he refers simply to it as "'the book,'" "short and jumbled and jangled . . . because there is nothing intelligent to say about a massacre." Of course, by speaking of his novel as jumbled, Vonnegut is not implying that the structure is unplanned and truly meaningless, that the novel is poorly thought-out or unintelligible, or that *Slaughterhouse-Five* is the work of a moral cynic and aesthetic nihilist [one who advocates destruction]. For the narrator adds in strong and unequivocal language a statement indicating that his abhorrence of war is absolute and unqualified, having told his "sons that they are not *under any circumstances* to take part in massacres, and that the news of massacres of enemies is not to fill them with satisfaction or glee" (my italics). Chaotic though the book may appear, it was neither conceived nor put together indifferently, at least in its final form. On the contrary, the apparently haphazard movement of the novel, the purposeful violation of normal chronological sequence, and the absence of conventional attitudes regarding the subject matter, are all purposefully inserted to prevent the reader from emerging from the work with a comfortable sense that moral order has been restored with the ending of the war, or that the factors that precipitated the carnage have been resolved or eradicated.

Conveying the Persistent Madness of War

The narrator-author has also come to see that almost all historical war novels distort the truth in conveying the impression that objective order and rationality prevail, just because various occurrences such as the events of World War II can be arranged on the basis of their chronological sequence. Even acknowledging the premise that a war has a beginning, a middle, and an end in a novel could detract from our ability to comprehend fully the actual madness behind it. To prevent all of this from happening in his own war novel, Vonnegut tampers throughout with temporal structure, presents us with a non-hero [Billy Pilgrim] so weak and passive it is impossible not to regard him with ambivalence, and denies this figure even the ability to remain rooted in causal time. But Billy's inability to put the events of time forever behind him is a trait shared by the reader of *Slaughterhouse-Five*, who is also at the mercy of the "Tralfamadorian" [a theory of time advocated by the inhabitants of the planet Tralfamadore] structure of the novel as engineered by the author, where all key events—the bombing of Dresden, the death of Edgar Derby, etc.—are repeated again and again. That the reader is never allowed to lose sight of these events reinforces what is surely one of Vonnegut's main themes in the novel: that since man's destructive nature is always with us, events should never be forgotten, if we are ever to stand a chance of preventing them from recurring.

Why the Innocent Suffer

Donald E. Morse

Donald E. Morse has served as a professor of English and rhetoric at Oakland University and as a visiting professor at the University of Debrecen, Hungary. He has published two books on Kurt Vonnegut.

In the following viewpoint, Morse argues that Slaughterhouse-Five *raises the same question with which Job challenged God in the Old Testament: Why do bad things (like the bombing of Dresden) happen to innocent people? Departing from the interpretation of most critics, Morse contends that Vonnegut does accept the Tralfamadorian philosophy: "There is no why." Using the words of Jesus from the Bible, Vonnegut affirms that "Rain falls on the just and unjust alike." Yet he conveys in his novel that sometimes goodness prevails and that in the worst of times, good people persist. War may be unstoppable, but at least, Vonnegut believes, publishing the truth about a massacre may be a way to change human values.*

Vonnegut wrote *Slaughterhouse-Five* as Joseph Heller wrote *Catch-22*, looking back on the Second World War from a vantage point of twenty to twenty-five years. Unlike Heller, however, what he found to criticize was not "everyone cashing in"—in an ironic moment he even admitted that "one way or another, I got two or three dollars for every person killed [in Dresden]. Some business I'm in"—but rather [he] chose to focus on the brutal, excessive destruction done in the name of goodness, justice, and Mom's apple pie.

Like Job, the Innocent Suffer

In his introduction to the novel, Vonnegut applauds Lot's wife, who in the Old Testament was turned into a pillar of salt

Donald E. Morse, "Vonnegut as Messenger: *Slaughterhouse-Five*," *Kurt Vonnegut.*

for daring to witness the destruction of Sodom and Gomorrah, the infamous cities on the plain. "I love her for that," says Vonnegut, "because it was so human." By looking back at the destruction of Dresden, Vonnegut reminds readers that, even in the best of causes against the worst of enemies, human beings have done and apparently will continue to commit the most unimaginable of atrocities. Why? In the Book of Job in the Old Testament, Job long ago found the answer to that question and Vonnegut repeats it for today's readers: "Why?" Why not? Because a person is good does not mean that he or she will escape evil or that he or she is incapable of doing evil. Job's expectation, that evil would not be visited upon a good or an innocent person, was as ill-founded a belief as Vonnegut's or anyone's might be. *Slaughterhouse-Five* suggests, therefore, that evil is beyond human understanding and that the destruction of the innocent and undefended is as common now as when Job bewailed his fate.

For much of his career as a writer and for half his career as a novelist, Kurt Vonnegut wrestled with the terrible moral issue of surviving the destruction of the unarmed city of Dresden in a firestorm in which "The city appeared to boil," leaving 135,000 dead in one night. Such massive destruction is almost beyond human imagining and certainly mind-numbing. About such devastation in *Slaughterhouse-Five*, Vonnegut says:

> . . . I felt the need to say this every time a character died: 'So it goes.' This exasperated many critics, and it seemed fancy and tiresome to me, too. But it somehow had to be said.

> It was a clumsy way of saying what [French doctor and author Louis-Ferdinand] Celine managed to imply so much more naturally in everything he wrote, in effect: "Death and suffering can't matter nearly as much as I think they do. Since they are so common, my taking them so seriously must mean that I am insane. I must try to be saner."

But how? Having survived the firebombing and what may well be the largest single massacre of European civilian population ever, he returned home after being repatriated as a prisoner of war. Like many of his contemporaries, he had interesting stories to tell of the war and the camaraderie he experienced, but again and again he failed to find the right medium for his message about the massacre and whatever it might mean. Unable to passively accept the destruction, he asked the questions all survivors ask, "Why me?" "Why was I allowed to survive?" And parallel to that question, there were all the others: "How could this terrible destruction have been allowed to happen?" "How could human beings do such awful things to one another?" In novel after novel, Vonnegut tries to deal with these questions directly or indirectly. . . .

The Eternal Question of "Why Me?"

In *Slaughterhouse-Five*, Vonnegut at last discovers a way of dealing artistically and personally with "death and suffering" by shifting his perspective from that of human beings to that of God or, in this instance, to that of the Tralfamadorians [beings from a planet in another galaxy]. When Billy Pilgrim finds himself in the Tralfamadorian zoo, he asks: "Why me?" The answer he receives both puzzles and instructs him:

> "That is a very *Earthling* question to ask, Mr. Pilgrim. Why *you*? . . . Why *anything*? Because this moment simply is. . . .
>
> Well, here we are, Mr. Pilgrim trapped in . . . this moment. There is no *why*."

This Tralfamadorian perspective, which Vonnegut adopts, is very similar to God's as pictured in the Book of Job. In the prologue to the Book of Job, messengers come to Job bringing news of horrendous destruction. The first one reveals that all his servants have been killed; the second that his sheep have been destroyed by fire from heaven; the third that nomads

In the Old Testament, Lot's wife is turned to a pillar of salt after she looks back on the destruction of Sodom and Gomorrah. In his introduction to Slaughterhouse-Five, *Vonnegut praises her courage and humanity, drawing a parallel between her act and his own attempt to capture the atrocities of Dresden in his novel.* Hartmann Schedel/Corbis.

have carried off his camels and killed his herdsmen; and the fourth brings the worst news of all: a hurricane suddenly killed all his sons and daughters. Naturally Job is heart-stricken. He rends his clothes and goes and sits on the village dunghill in deep mourning. While there, he receives visits from three friends who attempt to comfort him with conventional wisdom arguing that evil occurs because a person has done evil. Job claims, rightly, that he is innocent, God-fearing, and has done only good. The second friend contends that evil occurs because a person neglects to perform certain required ceremonies or religious duties, and if only Job will repent and perform them, all will be well. But again Job says that he is a model of piety and has left no ceremony unobserved nor any duty unperformed. The third friend then argues that evil never occurs without a reason, and, therefore, if destruction has been visited upon Job, then, that is ipso facto proof that Job is indeed guilty of something. If he will but "search his heart" to discover his mistake and repent of it, then, all will be well. But Job has done nothing wrong.

The Rain Falls on Just and Unjust Alike

As Jesus was to say a few centuries later, "The rain falls on the just and the unjust," and because a hurricane destroys people or property is no reason to believe such people were guilty of any wrong-doing. Nature is notoriously neutral and is, therefore, an unreliable guide to human goodness or evil. Writing "A Letter to the Next Generation" in an "Open Forum" series of advertisements sponsored by Volkswagen [in *The Wall Street Journal*], Vonnegut concludes by giving a lengthy list of natural disasters and saying: "If people think Nature is their friend, then they sure don't need an enemy." In other words, do not look to Nature for moral guidance.

Job's tragedy is that he is a good man who experienced great evil—exactly as Dresden was a "good" city, an "open" [off limits as a target], unarmed civilian city whose architectural beauty was legendary. Yet Dresden was destroyed though undefended "to hasten the end of the war," as Job's innocent sons and daughters were destroyed to "teach Job a lesson." By the end of the book, Job accepts the imperfection of the world and his inability to account for the evil in it. As the man of faith, he also comes to accept the goodness of his Creator, although that goodness may not always be apparent in the less than perfect world in which he must live. He states simply, "I believe; help Thou mine unbelief," which is the heartfelt cry of all believers in a Deity.

Sometimes Goodness Prevails in a Cruel World

Vonnegut, as a rational atheist, can find none of the consolation that Job found in the answers of traditional faith. He can and does find some consolation, however, in accepting an imperfect world where the power of evil to destroy is real and often terrifying, but where the power of reason and goodness is also real and occasionally even wins out over evil. As a character in a Bertolt Brecht [German author] play says, "In the worst of times, there are good people." . . .

In his role as the "messenger to Job," besides dealing with the "commonness" of death, Vonnegut also attempts to account for unmotivated human suffering, such as that caused by the incineration of 135,000 people in Dresden, by pointing to the accidental nature of life. . . .

Suffering Is Not Connected to Goodness

In *Slaughterhouse-Five* there is no one using or abusing human history for any purpose whatsoever nor is anything or anyone in control. Rather than wrestle further with the issue of "purpose" or lack of it, Vonnegut replaces the question, "Why me?" with its twin question to which there is no reply: "Why not you?" Questions also posed in the conclusion of the Book of Job first by Elihu, then by God, as each asks Job in turn: "Why did you expect that your goodness would give you immunity from the effects of evil or from accidents of nature?" There is no such immunity for human beings. Good people suffer and bad people suffer since "The rain falls on the just and the unjust." Suffering, by itself, is no measure either of a person's evil—as Job's three friends had mistakenly maintained—nor of a person's goodness—as Job had assumed. Suffering simply is a part of this world and all human experience, and no divine force will interfere in human history to stop it: ". . . the little Lord Jesus/No crying He makes."

Goodness Is Its Own Reward

The thought behind Vonnegut's novel could, therefore, be called a challenging, if fairly orthodox, form of Judeo-Christian theology. No wonder school boards and other official bodies whose members rarely read, much less comprehend, the books which they ban or burn, have attacked it and once, at least, in Drake, North Dakota; "*Slaughterhouse-Five* was actually burned in a furnace by a school janitor . . . on instructions from the school commitee"! It threatened their comfortable view of the world and religion exactly as the Book of Job, the Old Testament Prophets, and Jesus's Sermon on the Mount did hundreds of years ago. In all these books, as in *Slaughterhouse-Five*, the terms "punishment" and "reward" it turns out, do not make a lot of sense from the human, but only from the divine perspective. In such a world, why would anyone do good rather than evil? A good person, according to the Book of Job and Judeo-Christian belief, is simply a good person and the only reason for being good rather than evil is because that is who and what a good person is; thus, a good person is someone who does good which is its own reward. Someone who is evil, on the other hand, is simply someone who does evil, which is its own punishment.

War and Innocence

None of Vonnegut's characters, including those in *Slaughterhouse-Five*, are evil, but they are rather human beings to whom accidents happen. Most are innocent. Vonnegut's father once said to him, ". . . you never wrote a story with a villain in it." Billy Pilgrim is neither [actor] John Wayne, riding into the sunset to save Western civilization from the Fascists, nor Jesus preaching the necessity of "doing good to those who do evil to you." . . . The identity of soldiers as children is also reflected in the subtitle of *Slaughterhouse-Five: or The Children's Crusade*, which links the great war to end all wars with one of the most futile, exploitive, cynical events in all of western European history: the Children's Crusade—a crusade [in 1212, in which children purportedly set off to fight Muslims and retake Jerusalem for the Christian Church] that never went anywhere and never accomplished anything, except to provide ample prey upon which all kinds of human vultures fed.

In *Slaughterhouse-Five* the soldiers in World War II, like the children on the crusade, had little or no idea about what they were doing and often did not know even where they were. It was the generals who planned such glorious operations as the destruction of Dresden. The reduction of a monument of human civilization, such as the city on the Elbe [River], to a pile of rubble overnight or the metamorphosis of hundreds-of-thousands of unarmed people into a "corpse factory" can, and, indeed, has happened in a world where "everything is permitted." In such a world, says Ivan Karamazov in [Russian writer Fyodor Dostoevsky"s] *The Brothers Karamazov*, the issue is not whether to believe in God or not; it is the horror of the power of evil. Yet, as [the character] Eliot Rosewater, who also "found life meaningless, partly because of what [he] ... had seen in war," says to Billy Pilgrim: "everything there was to know about life was in *The Brothers Karamazov* ... 'But that isn't *enough* any more.' ...'" And so perhaps all we can do is to follow [American poet] Theodore Roethke's advice, which Vonnegut quotes with approval, to "learn by going where [we] ... have to go." Dresden, one of the most beautiful of all the German, of all the European cities was obliterated in one night with virtually all the people living there. . . .

Changing Values by Writing

"If the slaughterhouse itself, from which the novel takes its title, was once a house of death, it became, paradoxically during the inferno of the Dresden firebombing, a house of salvation when it gave oxygen to its occupants rather than to the firestorm. Similarly, while Vonnegut's novel is an account of the worst massacre of unarmed civilians in modern Europe, it is also a plea for a change in values and attitudes which would make other such massacres impossible. One way it accomplishes this task is by making the massacre itself public knowledge, for the novel brought it back into living memory in a way that could not be ignored, a portion of American history which had never officially been acknowledged, and which had been either inadvertently or deliberately concealed. According to Vonnegut in the "twenty-seven-volume *Official History of the Army Air Force in World War Two* . . . there was almost nothing . . . about the Dresden raid, even though it had been such a howling success. The extent of the success had been kept a secret for many years after the war—a secret from the American people."

Social Issues
in Literature

CHAPTER 3

Contemporary Perspectives on War

Uncovering Military Secrets About the Deaths of Iraqi Civilians

Sarah Lazare and Ryan Harvey

Sarah Lazare and Ryan Harvey are writers and organizers with the Civilian Soldier Alliance.

In this viewpoint, Lazare and Harvey report that in July 2007, US forces fired on the enemy in Iraq, killing twelve civilians and wounding children. The action was in keeping with military strategy, which requires soldiers to fire at the enemy even if women and children will be killed. The episodes were kept secret by the military until WikiLeaks, an international organization that publishes otherwise unavailable information online, was able to secure and distribute 90,000 secret documents about the war, including what was called the "Collateral Murder" video. It shows US forces firing from helicopters, killing more than a dozen Iraqi civilians. The incident was the direct result of military training. One soldier revealed afterward that he initially thought the United States was there to help the Iraqi people, but that he quickly became disillusioned. In his words, the troops were out-terrorizing the terrorists. Another soldier says he was reprimanded for refusing the order to shoot into crowds.

One by one, soldiers just arriving in Baghdad were taken into a room and questioned by their commanding officers. "All questions led up to the big question," explains former Army Spc. [Specialist] Josh Stieber. "If someone were to pull out a weapon in a marketplace full of unarmed civilians, would you open fire on that person, even if you knew you would hurt a lot of innocent people in the process?"

Sarah Lazare and Ryan Harvey, "Wikileaks in Baghdad," *The Nation*, August 16-23, 2010. Reproduced by permission.

Military Expectations

It was a trick question. "Not only did you have to say yes, but you had to say yes without hesitating," explains Stieber. "In refusing to go along with the crowd, it was not irregular for somebody to get beat up," he adds. "They'll take you in a room, close the door and knock you around if they didn't like your answer," says former Army Spc. Ray Corcoles, who deployed with Stieber.

According to these former soldiers, this was a typical moment of training for Bravo Company 2-16 (2nd Battalion, 16th Infantry Regiment), the ground unit involved in the infamous "Collateral Murder" video, which captured global headlines when it was released in April [2010] by WikiLeaks, the online clearinghouse for anonymous leaks. (In late July WikiLeaks dropped another bombshell with its release of more than 90,000 secret US military documents from the war in Afghanistan, including detailed reports on Pakistani collusion with the insurgents—who have successfully used heat-seeking missiles against allied forces—US assassination teams, widespread civilian casualties from US attacks and staggering Afghan government incompetence and corruption.)

The graphic video from Baghdad shows a July 2007 attack in which US forces, firing from helicopter gunships, wounded two children and killed more than a dozen Iraqis, including two Reuters [a global news agency] employees and the father of those children. The video quickly became an international symbol of the brutality and callousness of the US military in Iraq. What the world did not see is the months of training that led up to the incident, in which soldiers were taught to respond to threats with a barrage of fire—a "wall of steel," in Army parlance—even if it put civilians at risk.

On Military Instructions

Now three former soldiers from this unit have come forward to make the case that the incident is not a matter of a few bad-apple soldiers but rather just one example of US military protocol in the occupations of Iraq and Afghanistan, where excessive acts of violence often stem from the chain of command. This comes at a time when the top brass in Afghanistan are speaking openly of relaxing the rules of engagement. After Gen. [General] Stanley McChrystal's recent [June 23, 2010] ouster for publicly criticizing the Obama administration, his successor, Gen. David Petraeus, has asserted that military protocol in Afghanistan should be adjusted because of "concerns" about "the application of our rules of engagement," a move that critics fear will cause civilian deaths to skyrocket.

The story that Stieber, Corcoles and former Army Spc. Ethan McCord tell provides crucial background for the incident that WikiLeaks made famous. Bravo Company 2-16 deployed to Iraq in February 2007 during the "surge" ordered by [President] George W. Bush. Their spring arrival in New Baghdad, a dangerous neighborhood in eastern Baghdad bordering Sadr City, coincided with the start of the deadliest three-month period for US forces during the Iraq War.

Terrorizing the Terrorists

"I had the idea that I was going over there to help the Iraqi people—you know, freedom and democracy," says McCord, an expectation that Stieber and Corcoles say they shared. They learned quickly that the reality was very different. All three of these former soldiers describe a general policy of, in McCord's words, trying to "out-terrorize the terrorists" in order to establish power in a neighborhood that clearly did not want US troops there. The next months would be spent raiding houses, responding to sniper fire and IEDs [improvised explosive devices], and, as Corcoles says, "driving around just waiting to be shot at." All of them would witness the abuse, displacement and killing of Iraqi civilians.

When Bravo Company 2-16 arrived in New Baghdad to establish its Combat Outpost (COP) in an old factory, hundreds of angry residents gathered in protest. In grainy video footage brought back by McCord, residents can be seen converging around the soldiers and chanting, and McCord is seen standing in front of the crowd with his weapon drawn. Corcoles, behind the camera, was guarding the gate of the new post. "The first sergeant told me to shoot anyone who tried to rush the soldiers outside the gate," he says. Some Iraqis were then dragged inside, beaten and questioned. When the crowds dispersed, construction crews came in to begin building a wall around the new post. To clear the area, the military forced people to leave. "We were kicking people out of their homes," says McCord. "People who didn't want to move, we would basically force them to move . . . pretty much making them leave at gunpoint."

From then on the violence escalated. Corcoles describes the first IED death his unit suffered. "We did a mission that night till like midnight, and we were actually just sitting down. . . . I hadn't even got three or four drags off my cigarette and an IED went off. . . . We watched the Humvee burn, but we didn't realize [someone] was still in it."

The IED attacks left the soldiers angry and scared. McCord recalls one mission to impose curfews. Earlier that day, a popular soldier had died in an IED attack, and the troops took it out on the Iraqis. "There were a lot of people who got beat up that night," he says bluntly. This anger was turned into policy by the chain of command. "We had just lost three guys to an IED when the battalion commander came out to the COP," says McCord. He went on to explain that the commander gave orders to shoot indiscriminately after IED attacks. . . .

Opening Fire on Everyone

"When one [IED] went off, you were supposed to open fire on anybody," says Stieber. "At first I would just fire into a field.

Then I wouldn't fire at all." He describes an IED that went off near a crowd of teenagers. "I said I wouldn't fire," even though "other people were firing," he recalls. Like Stieber, Corcoles describes incidents in which he purposely aimed his gun away from people. "You don't even know if somebody's shooting at you," he says. "It's just insanity to just start shooting people." Stieber pointed out that in incidents like these, it was very rare for US military vehicles to stop to help the wounded or assess how many people had been injured or killed.

Stieber was intimidated and reprimanded by his command for refusing orders to shoot. "One time when I didn't fire, people in my truck were yelling at me for the rest of the mission. When we got back, one or two leaders got up in my face and kept yelling at me and stuff," he says. The command eventually stopped sending him on missions as a gunner, and Stieber says he "faced a lot of criticism for it." Corcoles saw this too. "One night our truck got hit by an IED and Josh didn't fire, and another soldier didn't fire," he says. "And they were getting yelled at: 'Why aren't you firing?' And they said, 'There's nobody to fire at.'"

Corcoles recalls another "wall of steel" incident: "Our first sergeant was with us, and after we got hit by an IED, people started shooting everywhere, and they were also actually shooting at him." He explains that his sergeant happened to be within range of indiscriminate fire coming from US soldiers. After almost getting shot by the soldiers, "our first sergeant told us not to do this anymore," says Corcoles.

Excessive acts of violence were woven, into daily missions, house searches and prisoner detention, says McCord. "This one time, in the summer of 2007, we were in a barbershop and my platoon leader was asking the barbershop owner about the local militia," he says. "The interpreter kept saying the owner didn't know anything. The platoon leader said, 'He is f---ing lying,'" says McCord, explaining that it was always assumed that Iraqis who said they didn't know anything were lying. "I remember my platoon leader punching him in the face. When [the barbershop owner] went to ground, he was kicked by others in the platoon. Many other Iraqis were in there to get their hair cut. They were up against the wall watching him get kicked."

McCord says that when others in his unit saw this kind of behavior condoned by the leadership, they followed suit. He describes multiple instances in which soldiers abused detainees or beat people up in their houses. In one case, he says, someone was taken from his house, beaten up and then left on the side of the road, bloodied and still handcuffed.

Civilian Carnage

In this setting, the "Collateral Murder" incident does not stand out as a drastic departure from the norm. That morning, Corcoles and McCord prepared for a "Ranger dominance" mission, "a clearing mission to basically go through every house, top to bottom, from one end of town to the next," says Corcoles. Stieber, who had been pulled off these missions because of his refusal to fire at crowds, was not with them this time. For the rest of the unit, what started as another day of house searches became a four-hour battle with militia members, say Corcoles and McCord. McCord was searching houses near Corcoles when he heard two Apache helicopters open fire nearby. He knew these helicopters were assigned to guard forces on the ground, so he knew something serious was occurring. "I heard over the net that we needed to move to that position," he recalls. He ran four or five blocks to the scene. "I was one of the first six dismounted soldiers to arrive there."

"It seemed unreal," says McCord, who describes running up and "seeing the carnage of what used to be human beings on the corner." A passenger van sat nearby, pocked with bullet holes and littered with bodies. Corcoles arrived on the scene shortly after McCord, who soon discovered two critically wounded children in the van and was able to pull them to safety. These moments would later be broadcast around the world in harrowing detail. McCord is seen in the video rushing wounded children away from the van. Photos that McCord took at the scene show mangled corpses lying in the road and one of the children, crouched in the front seat of the van next to a dead body.

Immediately following the incident, McCord was threatened and mocked by his commanding officer for pulling the children from the van. He says his platoon leader "yelled at me that I need to quit worrying about these 'motherf---ing kids' and pull security." McCord later approached a staff sergeant and told him he needed mental healthcare after the incident.... "I was told there would be repercussions." Fearing punishment, McCord did not ask again.

After conducting an internal investigation, the military cleared the unit of any wrongdoing. An "Investigation into Civilian Casualties Resulting from an Engagement on 12 July 2007 in the New Baghdad District of Baghdad, Iraq" found that "the proceedings comply with legal requirements" and "contain no material errors or violate any individual's substantial rights." The US Central Command refused several requests for an interview. And now Army intelligence analyst Bradley Manning, who is accused of leaking the video to WikiLeaks, is facing heavy charges punishable under the Espionage Act. The 22-year-old was transferred to Kuwait for a military trial that could lock him away in prison for decades. ...

McCord would return home early, suffering long-term injury from IED attacks that left him with a shattered lower spine and traumatic brain injury (TBI). He says the military at first tried to deny him treatment but eventually agreed to grant him back surgery after civilian tests showed serious injury. Despite TBI and severe post-traumatic stress disorder (PTSD), McCord says the military refused to grant him a medical discharge and instead discharged him with a preexisting personality disorder, a distinction that precludes him from receiving disability benefits from the military.

The three soldiers returned to the United States disillusioned with the war they had once volunteered to fight. "From my experiences in Iraq, we shouldn't even be in these countries fighting wars. This is a war of aggression, of occupation. There is nothing justifiable to me about this war," says Mc-Cord. "And this isn't someone sitting back saying 'I think' or 'I believe.' This is from someone who was there."

Soldiers Speaking Out Against the War

Three years after their deployment to Iraq, these former soldiers were forced to confront that war when the WikiLeaks video was thrust into the limelight. They watched as the familiar scene became a media sensation, making international headlines and raising the ire and disgust of people around the world.

By this point, Stieber, now 22, had become an outspoken peace activist. When he heard about the video, he was in the midst of planning a speaking tour with a man from Iraq with the goal of "showing that we have more in common with the people we're told are our enemies than those telling us who our enemies are," he says. After WikiLeaks posted the video, Stieber e-mailed several people from his former unit explaining that he was going to speak out about the incident. Mc-Cord, now 34 and raising two children, and Corcoles, 35 and raising a child, have both decided to join Stieber's effort.

The three have decided to go public to let the world know the context behind the acts caught on film. "If people don't like that video, then the entire system needs to be re-examined, and I think it illustrates why we shouldn't put soldiers in that situation," insists Stieber. Corcoles, now suffering from severe PTSD, says he wants the public to understand that "war kills civilians first." He says, "I think Americans . . . need to take responsibility. If you pay taxes, you pay for that soldier's wage. You're just as guilty as the soldier pulling the trigger."

"What was shown in the Wikileaks video only begins to depict the suffering we have created," reads an open letter from McCord and Stieber to the Iraqis who were injured or lost loved ones in the July 2007 attack. "From our own experiences, and the experiences of other veterans we have talked to, we know that the acts depicted in this video are everyday occurrences of this war: this is the nature of how US-led wars are carried out in this region."

Of course, these are not the first soldiers to break the silence about the rules of engagement in the ongoing wars in Iraq and Afghanistan. At the March 2008 Winter Soldier hearings in Maryland, more than fifty veterans and active-duty service members publicly testified about the orders they were told to carry out in these countries, sharing stories of excessive violence, as well as of abusive and threatening treatment they endured from their superiors.

The three former soldiers say they support the decision to leak these videos to the public. "Avoiding talking about what's going on is going to make us continue making the same mistakes and not learning our lesson," insists Stieber. About the most recent WikiLeaks revelations, Stieber says, "People all over the world have been confronted once again with the realities of the wars in Iraq and Afghanistan," adding that the latest release "confirms what veterans like Ethan, Ray and I, and so many other veteran witnesses, have been talking about."

But the occupations drag on, with President Obama continuing a Bush-era plan that will leave 50,000 "noncombat" troops in Iraq until at least the end of 2011. And top military brass have suggested that the August 31 deadline for withdrawal of "combat" troops may be extended. Meanwhile, Obama is sending 30,000 more troops to Afghanistan, bringing the total force there to more than 100,000, in what is now the longest war in US history. June was the deadliest month for NATO [North Atlantic Treaty Organization, a military alliance of European and North American countries] forces in Afghanistan, with 102 deaths, and as of press time July had become the second deadliest, with seventy-eight deaths.

All three soldiers say they hope Americans will learn the right lessons from the WikiLeaks video. "We acknowledge our part in the deaths and injuries of your loved ones as we tell Americans what we were trained to do and what we carried out in the name of 'god and country,'" write McCord and Stieber in their open letter. "The soldier in the video said that your husband shouldn't have brought your children to battle, but we are acknowledging our responsibility for bringing the battle to your neighborhood, and to your family. We did unto you what we would not want done to us."

"Our heavy hearts still hold hope that we can restore inside our country the acknowledgment of your humanity, that we were taught to deny."

Two Wars: Physical and Psychological

Stu Weber

Stu Weber is a minister, chaplain, author, and Vietnam special forces veteran with a particular interest in the plight of soldiers returning from war in the Middle East.

In the following selection, minister Weber writes about the wounds that soldiers suffer in war. His essay was written as a postscript to an autobiography by Nate Self, a veteran of wars in Afghanistan and Iraq. Weber says that there is a dark side to soldiering that those who have not been in battle can never understand. Self, whom Weber met in 2003 after his deployment in Afghanistan, had been in one of the most brutal firefights there and experienced the loss of "true friends, fellow soldiers, his brothers." After their meeting Self was again deployed, this time to Iraq. Weber contends that every soldier fights two wars: the physical war and the inner war. Something within the combatant dies after the battle. Weber explains that Self continues his life with a "hole in his heart."

"*T*o those who have fought for it, freedom has a flavor the protected can never know."

I'm not sure who made that statement, but it rings true. That's the bright side of soldiering, the good news—a quiet gratitude for life, lodged deep within a soldier's soul. Beauty, innocence, peace, family, faith, and the simple joys of life possess an extra measure of fragrance and flavor for those who have risked everything to defend them.

But soldiering has a dark side, too.

Stu Weber, "Afterward," *Two Wars: One Hero's Fight on Two Fronts-Abroad and Within*, by Nate Self. Tyndal House, 2008. Copyright © 2008 Tyndal House. All rights reserved. Reproduced by permission.

The old Negro spiritual says it well: "Nobody knows the trouble I've seen." Many servicemen and women who have logged time in combat would say the same thing. *Nobody knows. Nobody gets it. Nobody has any idea what it's like.*

Nobody, that is, except another soldier.

Where there is a battle, there are wounds, and where there are wounds, there are scars—scars of the body and scars of the soul. In one sense, this is the story of every soldier who has lived through the shock and violence of combat. At some point in the last fifty years or so, the long-term effects of such battles acquired a label. You've probably heard it kicked around at one time or another: Post-Traumatic Stress Disorder, or PTSD. . . .

They pay a heavy price. Some pay the last full measure and give their lives for us. Others are wounded, some severely so. Still others escape without physical wounds. But not one is untouched. And not one returns from combat the same person who entered it.

Nate Self and his platoon of brothers acquitted themselves with valor, honor, and sacrifice on as harsh a battlefield as you can imagine. But the story is not yet complete. The "journey back" to life and living, after staring death and dying in the face, is a long one. . . .

In the spring of 2002, I began devouring stories coming out of the conflict in Afghanistan. My heart was especially drawn to the superb work of our Special Forces troopers and our Rangers [elite army troops]. In particular, a desolate patch of high-altitude real estate called Takur Ghar held my attention. Whisked into a fierce firefight to rescue a Navy SEAL [Sea, Air, and Land Team] who had fallen out of the back of his helicopter, these men had stared "the elephant" of combat square in the eye.

My heart was with them. I could feel it.

The battle that Nate and his platoon fought may very well have been one of the longest single firefights in our Global

War on Terror. And it may hold yet another distinction—as the only infantry battle in our nation's history fought at or above ten thousand feet.

Nate Self in One of the Worst Wars in Afghanistan

I first met Nate Self in March 2003, about a year after his baptism on that mountaintop of ice and fire. I had taught a seminar and had spoken at a chapel service at Fort Leavenworth, Kansas. After the service, a strapping young captain, the epitome of America's finest and a student in the Army's Combined Arms Staff Services School, approached me. From the moment we began conversing, I sensed a palpable depth in the man. After a few minutes, in almost a whisper, he said, "I was the platoon leader of the QRF [quick reaction force] on Takur Ghar a year ago."

It took my breath away! I wanted to probe but held myself back. I knew he'd been through the most soul-stretching experience a man can face. So I walked carefully into our conversation, not wanting to hurt or embarrass this American hero in any way. I didn't want to go where he didn't want to go. I felt for him both a sense of awe and an overriding compassion. He had survived the worst that war has to offer—the loss of true friends, fellow soldiers, his brothers.

Redeployed and Having Family Problems

I went back to Oregon, half a continent away, and Nate deployed to war again, this time to Iraq. Nate and I stayed in touch after the seminar, occasionally talking by phone or e-mailing. Even after he left the Army, we stayed in touch. In one of those conversations, he made an offhand comment that I should have picked up on.

"We're experiencing some family stress because of all this."

Of course, I thought. *He's in the wake of it. The aftermath of an experience like that must be devastating.* It's been a part of every war, this near cousin to shell shock and battle fatigue. It's always the next big conflict that every combat veteran faces after returning home to civilian life.

I let Nate's comment about "family trouble" slip by, not knowing what to do with it. Did he want feedback? Was this a call for help? Should I, as a pastor and friend, have simply waded in? Because I didn't hear a direct invitation to get involved, I held back. I was more worried about wounding this young warrior's pride than responding to a need I understood all too well. Over time, I would learn that pride—the unhealthy kind that turns help away—was not an issue for Nate Self.

Along the way, Nate sent an e-mail that said very simply, with no fanfare, "By the way, Stu, NBC's *Dateline* is doing a special on Takur Ghar on June 11." I marked that date on my calendar and made sure I wouldn't be disturbed on the night it aired.

For me, the program was riveting. It was an account of that brutal, heartbreaking battle on Takur Ghar—but that's not where it stopped. The program went on to probe deeper into the hearts of Nate and Julie Self. Here was a young American soldier and his wife dealing with the burden of a deadly fight that had been won on the other side of the world but had come home to Texas to be fought in a different way.

My heart ached for them. I had to talk to Nate. I wanted to get them away from this broken world—if only for a day or two. I wanted that magnificent woman, Julie, to find her man again. I wanted them to experience some kind of oasis in the emotional desert of these overpowering post-traumatic storms. Just as Nate and his men had refused to leave that SEAL alone to fight his own battle, I could not bear the thought of Nate and Julie having to fight this second war alone.

The soldier's core value of leaving no man behind pulled hard at me. But I was half a continent away, tied up with a million details as pastor of a large church. How could I become meaningfully involved in this couple's life?

Then a thought struck me. It seemed crazy at first, but once it had occurred to me, I couldn't put it out of my mind. My wife, Linda, and I have access to a tiny log cabin in the Wallowa Mountains of northeast Oregon. It was built after World War II by a young veteran who came home from the war and lived there with his wife for half a century. Perhaps it could serve, at least for a few days, as a respite for another battle-weary soldier and his equally weary wife. . . .

I called Nate to simply express my love for him and Julie. And I invited them to take a minivacation and visit us in Oregon . . . escaping to our rustic little retreat in the Wallowa Mountains.

And they said yes.

When Nate and Julie flew in to Portland on a Friday evening, Linda and I instantly fell in love with them. We felt as if we were meeting our own adult children for the first time. We took them to our favorite seafood restaurant on the banks of the wide Columbia River and talked nonstop for hours. . . .

And we reflected on Nate's epiphany in Afghanistan, that he had not only a story to tell but also a message to steward: that a man today . . . can be both a physical warrior and a spiritual warrior at the same time. That the two are not exclusive. That neither compromises the other. . . .

Two Wars

Every combat warrior fights two wars. For the soldier, the sheer shock of combat is traumatic enough, but the anguish of losing his bearings in its wake may prove to be even more troublesome. Eventually, the battlefield falls silent. But its horrible echoes do not. And for the war that follows—the inner war—there is no training. It's like throwing a dime-store compass into a room full of magnets. Where is north? What's up, what's down? It is this loss of direction and basic instincts which most typifies the horror of post-traumatic stress.

Though the post-combat soldier may appear to be fully alive to those around him, something inside of him has died. The life he lived and the man he thought he was seem more like mirages than reality. How does he make decisions or move forward when he can't even grapple with his present location? It's a scary thing to be lost in the woods; it's much more terrifying to be lost inside yourself.

Nothing is normal anymore. And "normal" people who have no experience of similar trauma themselves can only stand back, it seems, and question the soldier's sanity. As the inner disorientation compounds itself, a dizzying downward spiral accelerates. And sometimes it erupts in sudden and irrational anger.

Where did that thought come from? Did I just say that? Why did I just do that? Where is this coming from?

Some have described it as a perpetually shuffling deck of cards. Just when the soldier thinks he's got a hand he can play, something or someone scrambles the deck.

Flashbacks. Confusion. Depression. Anxiety. Anger. . . .

It's as if every combat soldier lives with a hole in his heart. And though that hole is survivable, it seems to draw the soldier away from others and into a lonely place of isolation. It is this growing sense of aloneness that is most destructive.

Casualties of the Mind

Heidi Vogt

Heidi Vogt is a reporter for the Associated Press.

In the following selection, Vogt records the memories of four soldiers whose outpost in Afghanistan was attacked by the Taliban on October 3, 2009. Each continues to relive the battle. Ty Carter hears shots whenever he closes his eyes at night, recalling the moment when he was ordered not to rescue a fellow soldier who was crying to him for help. Ty says he became a zombie, refusing to talk to anyone and wearing dark glasses to warn people away. Jonathan Hill's reaction has been unrelenting anger. He had to put his fellow soldiers' bodies into body bags. Shane Courville also had to collect the bodies of soldiers that day; he talks about how they ran out of bags. After several deployments, his troubled marriage ended. Daniel Rodriguez has seen his friend die every day since the incident. He refuses counseling from someone who has never experienced combat.

Forward Operating Base Bostick, Afghanistan—More than nine months after one of the deadliest battles ever waged by U.S. forces in Afghanistan, the men of Bravo Troop, 3rd Squadron, 61st Cavalry are still fighting in—and with—their memories.

They cannot forget Oct. 3, 2009. On that day, 300 insurgents attacked two outposts in eastern Afghanistan manned by 72 soldiers, sparking a 12-hour fight. By nightfall, eight US soldiers were dead. Three days later, the outposts were closed.

Like so many of their comrades, they suffer from mental trauma. Nearly 20 percent of the 1.6 million troops who have

Heidi Vogt, "Causalities of the Mind," *Contra Costa Times,* July 25, 2010. Reproduced by permission.

returned from Iraq and Afghanistan reported symptoms of post-traumatic stress or major depression, according to a 2008 study by Rand Corp.

Only slightly more than half of those sought treatment. So, more and more, the army is bringing treatment to them, whether or not they ask for it.

After Oct. 3, most of the 18 men in Bravo troop—part of the Army's 4th Brigade Combat Team from Fort Carson, Colo.—met with counselors. Some went voluntarily, others under orders.

When they go, they have much to talk about. . . .

For Spc. Ty Carter, the hardest time is at night.

When he closes his eyes, gunshots from months ago echo through his head. He sees a wounded soldier dragging himself through the dirt on his forearms, shouting for help.

Only it isn't a nightmare—Carter doesn't sleep deeply enough in Afghanistan to dream. It's a memory of the excruciating 45 minutes when Carter had to watch that crawling man and do nothing, under strict orders from his superior officer.

Carter replays it over and over in his mind: Shrapnel hits Spc. Stephan Mace as he runs to a nearby building. Another soldier is also hit and killed immediately, going down like a spinning top. Mace, injured and unable to walk, crawls to his fallen comrade and shouts for help.

Carter—30 feet away—hears the cries. Under orders, he cannot go.

"You're no good to Mace if you're dead," the officer says.

Carter knows that sergeant probably saved his life. But even now, he feels the anger that welled up in him.

"It felt like nails in the stomach and acid on the brain," he says. "You have no idea what it feels like to watch a good man lie there in total pain, suffering. I knew that I could help him, I knew I could make it to him. But the answer, even after arguing, was still NO."

When Carter finally got the OK, he scooped Mace up and carried him to the aid station. To no avail—Mace died that night.

Carter, a towering 30-year-old from Antioch, says he couldn't keep his hands from shaking for days. He had trouble controlling his anger. A military psychologist and an Army chaplain suggested sleep aids, so he went on Ambien.

For weeks, he refused to talk with anyone. He skipped a mandatory group counseling session. He started wearing sunglasses inside the brightly lit mess hall so no one would bother him, and no one would see when his eyes welled up.

His platoon leader, Sgt. Jonathan Hill, ordered him into a private counseling session.

"He grabbed me and said, 'You of all people are going to go down there,'" Carter says. "Which he was totally right to do, because I was done. I couldn't hold any emotions in. I was a walking zombie."

Carter struggled in Afghanistan with the knowledge that setting up life again in the United States would be difficult. While home on leave, he carried around a copy of his statement about the attack so he wouldn't have to talk about it. Every time he told the story, he felt all the energy was sucked from him for a day and a half.

"Just sitting in a bar listening to people talk causes me to clench my hands," he says. "So much stress over who is seeing who, or the traffic, or how a server got someone's coffee wrong. Guys causing fights over someone looking at their girlfriend wrong. Useless!"

Hill, the sergeant, has encouraged his soldiers to meet with psychologist Katie Kopp. He himself has met with her once a week in the months following the attack.

Kopp has taught him to write his emotions down in a journal. The first few times, he found himself writing about fellow soldiers with such anger and force that he nearly broke his pencil.

Hill is haunted by the memory of seeing another soldier die—and knowing that but for a few minutes, it would have been him. When he talks about what happened, his voice is calm, but he smokes cigarettes ceaselessly. The 38-year-old doesn't remove his sunglasses, and his hands fold and unfold nervously as if they have a troubled life of their own.

At 6 AM on Oct. 3, he woke up to an explosion and fire that turned his barracks into a clay oven. He ordered his 18 men to grab their weapons and get out.

Hundreds of militants with ammunition slung over their tunics were running down a dirt road toward the base. Mortar rounds hit every 15 seconds, and the smell of gunpowder hung heavy in the damp air. Hill felt bullets hit in front of his face and behind his head.

Another soldier, Sgt. Joshua Kirk, ran into a building first, while Hill stopped to grab some ammunition.

Then the building exploded.

Hill went for help. When he returned, others were carrying Kirk out of the building on a stretcher.

"He was pretty floppy. He had no life in him. His arms were just hanging off the stretcher. When I saw that, I pretty much gathered that he didn't make it," Hill says, his face strained with the effort of keeping his voice even.

Hill is certain that if he had been a few seconds quicker, he would have died too: "I was supposed to be right where he was."

He thinks about his two children—an 8-year-old girl and a 12-year-old boy—and how they could have grown up without a father.

Hill remembers vividly how he zipped three of his fellow soldiers into body bags that evening, and carried the heavy, lifeless sacks to a waiting helicopter.

"Having to put all those young soldiers in body bags," he starts, his voice trailing off. "That's a memory that's never going to go away."

Col. Thomas Hicklin, head of the US Army's Combat Stress Control Company Detachment, offers counseling to a soldier in Bagram, Afghanistan. According to a 2008 study by Rand Corp., nearly 20 percent of the troops who have returned from Iraq and Afghanistan reported symptoms of post-traumatic stress disorder or major depression. AP Photo/Wally Santana.

He has talked with Kopp about the attack, but had trouble sharing details with his wife when he was home on leave. He says he wanted to spare her the pain.

One night, after they put their children to bed, she asked what happened. He was curt: "It was a long, 12-hour battle. We had this many and we lost this many."

"She grew up in a military family as well," he says. "So she can do the math."

Staff Sgt. Shane Courville takes a different tack—he tries not to think about what happened.

"You block it out until you get home," he says.

When he does talk about it, he speaks flatly, his eyes looking straight ahead at the wall.

On that day, Courville was the one who got the bodies. Kirk was first. Courville remembers the call at the aid station that someone was down.

He ran, grabbed Kirk and carried him back.

The 28-year-old medic piled the first three bodies in a room off the aid station where he slept. Then he started putting them out on the porch outside the building. After the fourth dead body, he ran out of body bags and just lay them in the open air.

"Scusa came in dead. Griffin came in dead. Gallegos. Hardt. Thomson," he says.

Courville says that he'll deal with Afghanistan back in the States. He's gone through it before. This is his fourth deployment, including Afghanistan in 2003 and Iraq twice. After the first Iraq deployment, his wife made him visit a military psychologist because he was having nightmares and they were getting into fights—"the normal stuff," Courville says.

This time his wife won't be around. They separated in November, just a month after the Keating attack. He says she was cheating on him.

He planned to do the required counseling in the States, but not to seek more. Instead, he's got his own way of dealing with the aggression—he decided to ride a bull in rodeo. It's something he's been wanting to do since before he shipped off to Afghanistan.

Sgt. Daniel Rodriguez sees the face of a dying soldier when he tries to sleep.

"There's not a night that I go to sleep that I don't think about it," says Rodriguez, 22. "He was speechless. His eyes were open like he was trying to tell me something and it didn't come out. And he was gurgling. And I'm trying to pull him in and it just isn't happening, and it kicks in that there's nothing I can do for my friend."

When the explosion rocked the base, Rodriguez jumped up and ran to his post, the mortar pit.

He remembers muzzle flashes everywhere, looking like popcorn hitting around him.

As soon as he made it to the mortar pit, he saw Pvt. Kevin Thomson die—shot in the head as he passed in front of Rodriguez. He's seen it again in his mind many times since.

Rodriguez, who is on his second tour in three years, doesn't want his time in the military to define his life. After returning from Afghanistan, he plans to go to school: first junior college to save money, then on to a degree in business or nutrition.

Rodriguez, a small man with a young face, went through the required sessions with the psychologist, but says he doesn't plan to seek further counseling. He says it's unnecessary—he'll talk to friends and family.

With Rodriguez, it's hard to draw the line between practicality and bravado.

"They think all of us around are going to be serial killers within the next five years," he says. "When I get home and people automatically assume that I'm going to be crazy, I'm like no, I'm fine. Yeah, I've seen some (expletive), but I'm not going to snap.

"Either you're built for it or you're not," he says. "We've seen our friends killed in front of us. We've put them in body bags, and we're still strong."

He dismisses "combat stress"—counseling sessions—as perfunctory.

"So when you come back to here and you go to a combat stress from somebody who has a Ph.D. and what-not and has never set foot in harm's way, he's only giving you textbook criteria or a pill that will help you sleep better at night."

Kopp, the psychologist, hears that kind of thing a lot. So she tells them to help her understand what it was like. The way they tell the story often reflects how much they've come to terms with it.

Avoidance is typical. They don't make eye contact, or their leg starts bouncing. Their eyes look around. Sometimes their narrative jumps around in time, as if it's still all a jumble in their heads. Other times they detail a horrific battle without one sign of emotion.

"It's just completely flat. They tell you that their friend was killed in the same way that they'd tell you about their trip to the grocery store yesterday," Kopp says.

Kopp says each soldier's timeline is different. There's no predicting when a soldier will be ready to open up.

"Some people, it's going to hit them right away. Two days after, they were talking to me about trying to deal with it," she says. "Some of them still haven't come forward."

Child Soldiers

Michelle Steele

Michelle Steele writes for Vision, *a religious-based international journal, and its website, Vision.org.*

In this viewpoint, Steele pulls together information from multiple sources to report on child soldiers throughout the world. One source includes the memoirs of a boy abducted by the army in Sierra Leone. In 2008 the United Nations [UN] estimated that, at any given time, 250,000 boys and girls below the age of eighteen were fighting in wars throughout the world. Some are as young as five. Little girls are forced to fight in the front lines as well as serve as cooks and maids. It is accepted that they will be sexually assaulted by male members of the army. Children are desirable to armies because they are ignorant, obedient, and cheap. The army uses drugs to control them. The main form of recruitment is kidnapping. Many children continually hide to escape the army, but villages that do not deliver their quota of children are attacked. The challenge the survivors face is enormous. It takes months for these children, hardened as killers by the army, to withdraw from drugs and integrate back into society.

When you think of war, what images come to mind? Perhaps you see rows of uniformed soldiers marching in step, or tanks and armored vehicles traveling in convoy, or the US military's televised "Shock and Awe" precision bombings over Iraq. The reality, however, is that the majority of wars today are intrastate [within one country] conflicts fought with small arms. And the disturbing news, as reported in the "Child Soldiers Global Report 2008," is that wherever such conflicts take place, many of those fighting are children. Yet how often, when you think of war, do you picture a *child* brandishing an AK-47 assault rifle or a rocket-powered grenade launcher?

Michelle Steele, "Child Soldiers," *Vision.org*, Fall 2008. Reproduced by permission.

At least one such child's story has become widely known: *A Long Way Gone: Memoirs of a Boy Soldier* provides the moving firsthand account of Ishmael Beah's experiences as a child soldier in Sierra Leone. Separated from his family when their village was attacked by rebel forces, Beah for a while avoided abduction into the armed conflict that enveloped his country. Eventually, however, hunger and insecurity led him to join the government forces, who compelled him not only to fight against the rebel opposition but to perpetrate acts of extreme violence against innocent civilians along the way.

Children in Wars Around the World

While Beah's story is shocking, it is certainly not unique. He was just one of an estimated 250,000 boys and girls (according to current UN estimates) taking part in wars around the world at any given time over the last two decades. His book has increased awareness of the plight of children who are prematurely exposed to the harshest and most brutal experiences imaginable, including murder, mutilation and rape.

What Is a Child?

While the definition of childhood varies from culture to culture, the UN Convention on the Rights of the Child defines "child" broadly as "every human being below the age of 18 years." The 2007 Paris Principles interpret "a child associated with an armed force or armed group" as "any person below 18 years of age who is or who has been recruited or used by an armed force or armed group in any capacity, including but not limited to children, boys, and girls used as fighters, cooks, porters, messengers, spies or for sexual purposes. It does not only refer to a child who is taking or has taken a direct part in hostilities."

Most child soldiers are between the ages of 13 and 18, though many groups include children aged 12 and under. Beah, for example, fought alongside a 7-year-old and an 11-

year-old. The latter was mortally wounded by a rocket-propelled grenade, Beah recalls, and as the small boy lay dying in front of him, "he cried for his mother in the most painfully piercing voice that I had ever heard."

A May 2006 Africa Research Bulletin reported that "in states such as Angola, Burundi, Congo, the Democratic Republic of Congo, Rwanda, Sudan and Uganda, children, some no more than seven or eight years of age, are recruited by government armed forces almost as a matter of course," while rebel forces in Sierra Leone were known to recruit children as young as five.

According to the "Child Soldiers Global Report 2008" (produced by the Coalition to Stop the Use of Child Soldiers), 21 countries or territories around the globe had children engaged in conflicts between 2004 and 2007. Today there are child soldiers in many nations around the world, including the Central African Republic, Chad, Somalia, Uganda, Myanmar (Burma), Sudan, Iraq, Colombia and Sri Lanka. Both government and non-state forces in developed and developing countries are culpable. Developing countries embroiled in intrastate conflicts tend to use younger children in their desperation, but even the United Kingdom, the United States, Australia, Canada and New Zealand recruit youths as young as 17.

Girls in the Army

Girls not only fight on the front lines but provide domestic labor and serve as "wives." From the age of 13 they may be given to boy soldiers or adult commanders. They have no choice: those who refuse are killed or raped. Of course, many of them soon become mothers who must take on the added responsibility of providing food for their children. It's a grueling existence, and malnourishment, exhaustion and mistreatment take a high toll.

It's no wonder, then, that many of their babies don't survive. Some don't even survive birth itself. In "Child Soldiers: What About the Girls?" University of Montana researcher Dyan Mazurana and University of Wyoming professor Susan McKay assert that "the RUF's [Revolutionary United Front's] birthing practices in Sierra Leone included jumping on the abdomens of expectant girls and inserting objects into their vaginas to force the girls into labor well before they were properly dilated, or tying their legs together to delay birth if the forces needed to move quickly."

In addition to pregnancy and motherhood, repeated sexual assault can also lead to infection, disease (including HIV/ AIDS), uterine deformation, vaginal sores, menstrual complications, sterility and death, as well as to "shock, loss of dignity, shame, low self-esteem, poor concentration and memory, persistent nightmares, depression, and other post-traumatic stress effects." Mazurana and McKay stress the importance of treating these young women: "Because girls are the mothers and caregivers for future generations, their health has a critical impact on the overall health of a nation and its population."

A Ready Commodity

According to an Amnesty International report, "both governments and armed groups use children because they are easier to condition into fearless killing and unthinking obedience." Children are a cheap and plentiful resource for military commanders in need of a steady troop supply to war zones. Their underdeveloped ability to assess danger means they are often willing to take risks and difficult assignments that adults or older teenagers will refuse. Children are more impressionable than adults, and depending on their age and background, their value systems and consciences are not yet fully developed.

While children become involved with armed groups in a variety of ways, child-soldier expert Michael Wessells told *Vi-*

sion [magazine] that no choice is a "free choice" because it is typically grounded in dire circumstances, including poverty, starvation, separation from their families, physical or sexual abuse, or lack of livelihood or education. China Keitetsi, whose book *Child Soldier* relates her own story of life in an armed group, joined because of a difficult home situation. It's true that some children decide to enter conflicts voluntarily because they relate to the group's ideology, as in Palestine and Sri Lanka; but most feel they simply have no choice.

Kidnapping as a Recruitment Technique

The most distressing method of recruitment is without a doubt kidnapping. The Lord's Resistance Army (LRA) in Uganda has the worst record of abduction, stealing tens of thousands of children over the past decade alone. This has created the "night commuters" phenomenon, portrayed in the stirring picture book *"When the Sun Sets, We Start to Worry . . .": An Account of Life in Northern Uganda*. Its foreword states, "Each night in northern Uganda, more than 40,000 mothers, grandmothers and children leave their homes and travel many miles on foot to the main towns, seeking refuge from abduction by the LRA." In town they will sleep outside hospitals, churches and other public buildings. Seventy-year-old Elijah tells of his experience: "At night, my eight grandchildren sleep in the bush with no blankets. I don't know where they sleep, and they always choose a different spot. Not even your mother is supposed to know your hiding place. Rebels always force parents to show them where the children are hiding."

UNICEF [the United Nations Children"s Fund] reports that the LRA has abducted children as young as 5 but mostly between the ages of 8 and 16, often after killing their parents in front of them. The young "recruits" are then forced to march to southern Sudan. Those who can't carry their loads

A Sudanese Toposa man poses with his son and a semiautomatic weapon. In Sudan and other war-torn areas, children are introduced to violence as a way of life at an early age. Blickwinkel/Alamy.

or keep pace with the others are killed. Those who attempt escape are severely punished. Girls are routinely raped.

Ugandans may be at highest risk of abduction, but children in other nations have plenty to fear as well. In Bhutan, Burundi, Myanmar, El Salvador, Ethiopia and Mozambique, says Wessells, children have even been kidnapped while at school. And the "Child Soldiers Report 2008" notes that the same is true in Bangladesh and Pakistan. Warlords in Afghanistan and Angola's UNITA [National Union for the Total Independence of Angola] have employed a quota system in which they demand that villages each hand over a certain number of youths. Those villages that don't oblige are attacked.

Turning Kids into Killers

Military commanders use proven tactics to produce unquestioning obedience in these homesick children while transforming them into killers. New recruits are often forced to kill or perpetrate various acts of violence against others, including strangers, escapees or even members of their own village or family. Coercing the children to harm or kill people they know has the added benefit of discouraging them from attempting escape, as they know they will no longer be welcome back home.

Some groups also practice cannibalism, making young recruits drink the blood or eat the flesh of their victims. While recruits are often told "It will make you stronger," Wessells argues that the real motivation is to "force children to quiet their emotional reactions to seeing people killed and demolish their sense of the sanctity of life and their tendency to show respect for the dead."

In addition, drugs are administered to deaden the effects of conscience: amphetamines, crack cocaine, palm wine, brown-brown (cocaine mixed with gun powder), marijuana and tranquilizers help disengage the child's actions from any sense of reality. Children who refuse to take the drugs are beaten or killed, according to Amnesty International. One rehabilitation camp director told Wessells that recruits "would do just about anything that was ordered" when they were on drugs. . . .

After Combat

Children who are rescued from combat, or who survive until the conflict's conclusion, face an enormous challenge in trying to return to normal civilian life. . . .

The rehabilitation process includes drug withdrawal and psychological adjustment but also recovery from posttraumatic stress disorder, the symptoms of which include nightmares, flashbacks, aggressiveness, hopelessness, guilt, anxiety, fear and social isolation. . . .

According to Christian Children's Fund, a leading nonprofit organization involved in psychosocial interventions including the rehabilitation of former child soldiers, it can take as long as three years to be reintegrated into society. Beah spent eight months in a rehab facility before being placed with an uncle. It took him two months just to withdraw from the drugs, and several months passed before he could sleep at night without medication. It took even longer for him to recall early childhood memories as he grappled with flashbacks of his war experiences. As he gradually learned to trust adults again, he marveled at the workers' patience and their refusal to give up on their hardened and antagonistic charges. Beah recalls that his nurse Esther looked at him with the "inviting eyes and welcoming smile that said I was a child." After being stabbed, beaten or otherwise mistreated by the children, the staff would tell them, "None of these things are your fault."

For Further Discussion

1. Make an argument for Vonnegut's antiwar stance using positions he took in his life. See Reed, Rackstraw, and Casey and Bellamy.

2. How does war become a tool of civilization? See Lundquist and McCoppin.

3. In your opinion are Tralfamadore and time travel real, or are they figments of Billy's imagination? See Allen, Edelstein, and Tanner.

4. Does Vonnegut endorse or reject Tralfamadorian philosophy? See Tanner, and Merrill, and Scholl.

5. How does Vonnegut deromanticize war? See Schatt and Matheson.

6. Vonnegut asks the eternal question: Why do innocents suffer? How do you think he answers that question? See Morse.

For Further Reading

Humphrey Cobb, *Paths of Glory*. New York: Viking Press, 1935.

Stephen Crane, *The Red Badge of Courage*. New York: D. Appleton, 1895.

Joseph Heller, *Catch-22*. New York: Simon and Schuster, 1961.

Ernest Hemingway, *A Farewell to Arms*. New York: Charles Scribner's Sons, 1929.

James Jones, *The Thin Red Line*. New York: Charles Scribner's Sons, 1962.

Karl Marlantes, *Matterhorn: A Novel of the Vietnam War*. Berkeley: El León Literary Arts, 2009.

Kurt Vonnegut, *Cat's Cradle*. New York: Delacorte Press, 1963.

———, *God Bless You, Mr. Rosewater*. New York: Delacorte Press, 1965.

———, *Mother Night*. New York: Dell Publishing, 1961.

———, *The Sirens of Titan*. New York: Delacorte Press, 1959.

Bibliography

Books

Stephen E. Ambrose	*Citizen Soldiers: The U.S. Army from the Normandy Beaches to the Bulge to the Surrender of Germany.* New York: Simon and Schuster, 1997.
Kevin A. Boon, ed.	*At Millennium's End: New Essays on the Work of Kurt Vonnegut.* Albany: State University of New York Press, 2001.
Lawrence R. Broer	*Sanity Plea: Schizophrenia in the Novels of Kurt Vonnegut.* Ann Arbor, MI: UMI Research Press, 1989.
Peter Galbraith	*The End of Iraq: How American Incompetence Created a War Without End.* New York: Simon and Schuster, 2006.
Richard Giannone	*Vonnegut: A Preface to His Works.* Port Washington, NY: Kennikat Press, 1977.
Seth G. Jones	*In the Graveyard of Empires.* New York: W.W. Norton, 2009.
Donald E. Morse	*The Novels of Kurt Vonnegut: Imagining Being an American.* Westport, CT: Praeger, 2003.

Leonard Mustazza   *Forever Pursuing Genesis: The Myth of
                   Eden in the Novels of Kurt Vonnegut.*
                   Lewisburg, PA: Bucknell University
                   Press, 1990.

Daryl S. Paulson   *Haunted by Combat.* Westport, CT:
and Stanley   Praeger, 2007.
Krippner

Peter J. Reed   *Kurt Vonnegut, Jr.* New York: Warner
                   Paperback Library, 1972.

Periodicals

Martin Amis   "Kurt's Cosmos," *Observer*, vol. 3,
                   November 1985.

Lynn Buck   "Vonnegut's World of Comic
                   Futility," *Studies in American Fiction*,
                   vol. 3, 1975.

Richard Budtke   "Great Sorrows, Small Joys: The
                   World of Kurt Vonnegut Jr.,"
                   Crosscurrents, vol. 20, Winter 1970.

Alberto Cacicedo   "'You Must Remember This': Trauma
                   and Memory in *Catch-22* and
                   Slaughterhouse-Five," *Critique*, vol. 46,
                   2005.

Barry C. Chabot   "*Slaughterhouse-Five* and the
                   Comforts of Indifference," *Essays in
                   Literature*, vol. 8, 1951.

Leslie A Fiedler   "The Divine Stupidity of Kurt
                   Vonnegut," *Esquire*, September 1970.

Donald J. Greiner "Vonnegut's *Slaughterhouse-Five* and the Fiction of Atrocity," *Critique*, vol. 14, 1973.

Alfred Kazin "The War Novel from Mailer to Vonnegut," *Saturday Review*, vol. 6, February 1971.

Kevin Maurer and "Marines Tackle Mental Health," *Bay Area News Group*, August 26, 2010.
Julie Watson

Wayne McGinnis "The Arbitrary Cycle of *Slaughterhouse-Five*: A Relation of Form to Theme," *Critique*, vol. 17, 1975.

Maurice "*Slaughterhouse-Five*: Kurt Vonnegut's
O'Sullivan Anti-memoirs," *Essays in Literature*, vol. 3, 1976.

Philip M. Rubens "'Nothing's Ever Final': Vonnegut's Concept of Time," *College Literature*, vol. 6, Winter 1979.

Internet Sources

David Kupler "Like Wandering Ghosts," *Sun*, June 2008. www.thesunmagazine.org.

Index